RESILIENCE IN CONCRETE
The Thomas P. Murphy Design Studio Building

Carmen L. Guerrero

RESILIENCE IN CONCRETE
The Thomas P. Murphy Design Studio Building

Preface Rodolphe el-Khoury
Acknowledgements & Introduction Carmen L. Guerrero
Interviews Carmen L. Guerrero assisted by
Kalil Mella & Emily Nelms
Photography Peter Leifer & Cheryl Stieffel of Miami in Focus, Inc.
and Robin Hill of Robin Hill Photography

OSCAR RIERA OJEDA
PUBLISHERS

Table of Contents

10	**Acknowledgements** Carmen L. Guerrero	134-151	The Drawings
12	**Preface** Rodolphe el-Khoury	152-161	**With the Curtain-Wall Manufacturer:** Jose Daes
14-31	**Introduction** **A Perfect Space for Architecture Pedagogy** Carmen L. Guerrero	162-173	**With the University Project Manager:** Gary Tarbe
32-55	The Interiors	174-185	The Experience
56-87	**With the Architects:** Bernardo & Ray Fort-Brescia, including: Thomas Westberg	186	**Building Credits**
88-115	The Exterior	192	**Book Credits**
116-133	**With the Builder:** Thomas C. Murphy, Sean M. Murphy & Patrick E. Murphy including: Jason Anderson and Nick Duke		

Acknowledgements | Carmen L. Guerrero

Prior to 2016, as a faculty member I had no profound insight into the nature of overseeing a school's physical environment and planning for its future. To the extent that this situation has changed I primarily owe to Dean Rodolphe el-Khoury for trusting me in my appointment as Associate Dean of Strategic Initiatives and Physical Planning of the University of Miami School of Architecture. Since assuming this position, I have been amazed to discover the important role facilities play in running a successful architecture program. As an architect I realized, of course, that our physical surroundings can shape our experiences positively or negatively, but what I did not foresee was the tremendous impact they have on teaching, recruitment, research and school recognition. I also did not foresee the agility required for the job in moving from seemingly mundane, day to day logistics to higher level thinking about our physical environment.

I understood I had to immerse myself in learning about the history of the school's facilities and about the achievements, goals and unfinished projects of previous school leadership. In this pursuit I am grateful to colleagues such as Tom Spain, Elizabeth Plater-Zyberk, Rocco Ceo, Jorge Hernandez, Denis Hector and Carie Penabad for sharing the histories and their insight with me over the years. An understanding of the school's history has been invaluable in providing me with direction and knowledge as I tackle the present and future building projects on our campus.

The physical planning activities of the school do not only involve the school community but also other departments of the University. I have forged many wonderful internal and external relationships with expert colleagues in departments such as Facilities & Operations Planning who offer great support in all phases of building and renovation projects. Without them, campus projects would be extremely challenging or not possible. I worked very closely with Juan Rodriguez-Vela, Maggie Binmelis and Gary Tarbe during the planning and construction of the new Thomas P. Murphy Studio Building. I have learned a great deal from them and also from Jessica Brumley, current VP of Facilities Operations & Planning. Karina Alvarez from the Department of Development and Alumni Relations offered great support in connecting me with the interviewees as well as in facilitating image requests.

I appreciate the time and stories contributed by the most valuable players in the design and construction of the Murphy Studio Building such as Bernardo Fort Brescia, Ray Fort, Thomas Westberg, Thomas C. Murphy, Sean M. Murphy, Patrick E. Murphy, Nick Duke, Jason Anderson, Jose Daes and Technoglass for the cutting edge technology and Gary Tarbe for his impeccable project management. Without their expertise and contributions neither the building nor this book would have been possible.

I also recognize the efforts of former students Kalil Mella and Emily Nelms in organizing the content of the book and assisting with the interviews, photography and communications parts of the project. Their energy was invaluable and I believe largely due to having had the experience of working in the new studio building during the course of their education at the University of Miami.

Thanks to Peter Leifer and Cheryl Stieffel of Miami in Focus for granting me access to their fantastic photographs of the new building.

And on behalf of the school, once again I would like to thank the generous donors that made this transformative building possible; Thomas P. Murphy Jr. for the naming gift and Jose Daes and Technoglass for the spectacular glazed curtain wall.

Lastly I would like to mention that putting this book together has offered not only respite during this pandemic era but also a reminder of the impact great and resilient buildings can have on our lives both during good and more importantly, during challenging times.

A Perfect Space for Architecture Pedagogy

Carmen L. Guerrero

This Covid-19 era reminds us of the power a crisis has in revealing true human character and resilience. We have had to reinvent our normal modus operandi at home, in school, at work and in our social circles. Here at the UM School of Architecture we have reprogrammed and reinvented our existing buildings and spaces to be able to continue our work safely during the pandemic. We have experienced first-hand how crises can place our physical environment to the test by measuring its ability to adapt, accommodate and create new opportunities. The newest addition to our precinct, The Thomas P. Murphy Design Studio Building has redefined resiliency in so many ways beyond the environment.

The Thomas P. Murphy Design Studio Building, also known as the Murphy Studio, joined the school of architecture campus in pre-pandemic 2018. Since then, the exposed concrete and glass rectangular building capped with a swooping roof has transformed the school's physical, pedagogical, and social dimensions beyond expectations. It brought to the school a unique type of space for teaching, learning, and working that is in constant evolution. It is primarily the home of our incoming first-year design studios, our fabrication resources, and our printing labs, but very swiftly can be modified to accommodate workshops, charrettes, lectures, exhibitions and more. And many times, all these activities can run simultaneously, much like in a busy and vibrant urban piazza.

At a broader level, the location of the building has also transformed the University of Miami master plan, positioning the school of architecture in a more accessible and central location, and creating new connections with other parts of the campus and the city. What was once considered the back side of the architecture campus is now reframed as the front towards Ponce de Leon boulevard and the University Metrorail station. The new building has also changed the perceived distance between the different buildings that make up the architecture campus. Locations on the architecture campus, jokingly referred to as "Siberia", because they are not within the boundaries of the main plaza on the lake, are now reframed as another central area of the school, along one of the new promenades that culminate at the Murphy Building.

The impact of the Thomas P. Murphy Design Studio Building on the school's physical environment is not only due to site placement but also to its architectural qualities and its interior. On the exterior, the deep and protected terraces and the long fully glazed façades have expanded the building's interior towards the outdoors, providing the school with excellent views and easily accessible open-air spaces. From most everywhere inside the building, the tropical and lush landscape of the campus becomes part of the interior experience. The indoor activities can easily occupy these outdoor living spaces which have excelled in their role as classrooms, critique area, lecture space, exhibition space, collaborative workspace, and social interaction spaces. The orientation of these terraces and the depth of their overhangs create very desirable places to be throughout the year. During this pandemic era, these outdoor spaces have offered much needed respite to the school and the university community while providing ample space for safe and socially distant encounters.

Outdoor settings are not new to the Miami architecture school nor to South Florida. We have the privilege of being in a "locality where the greater part of the time may be spent comfortably outdoors, [where] the sharp contrast between being inside or outside is diminished to a minimum. In such a situation the outdoor living room spans the gap between actual inside and outside and draws, as it were, the outside into the [building] and the inside outdoors. This is an ideal living condition which adds color and variety as no other enhancement of existence may."[1] Tropical South Florida offers this unique situation.

The school's original buildings are organized around a rectangular open plaza on a lake and also around open green lawns and paved courts. These open-air spaces have long served as settings for drawing classes, design reviews, lectures, meet-

---

[1] *Whitworth, Henry P. The Outdoor Living Room. 1936, Florida, Architecture and Allied Arts.*

ings, events, informal encounters, etc. What was missing in the school's facilities were covered outdoor living spaces, where all these activities could continue in the shade and away from the rain. The Murphy Studio Building has enriched our campus with a variety of exterior spaces to work and congregate; some are open to the air and shaded by trees, others are open in full sun, some are partially protected, such as the Krier loggia, and others are more fully protected such as the Murphy building terraces.

The spatial variety is equally present with the type of interior spaces for the design studio courses on the architecture campus. Prior to the construction of the Murphy Studio Building, the design studios were confined to the spaces inside the existing post-war barrack type buildings which have shaped the architecture campus for years. These buildings originally served the university as campus housing since 1945. Nearly four decades later, in 1983, the School of Architecture became independent from the College of Engineering and was relocated to these buildings.

The spaces inside these linear post-war buildings, also known as the Marion Manley buildings, are organized as a series of rooms, with corridors, bathrooms, and closets on each floor, and with extensive glazing on the long façades. In the conversion from apartments to design studios, a few alterations have been made to gain larger open areas, but most of the spaces remain in their original room sizes. Up until the opening of the Murphy Studio Building, all our design studios were organized in the rooms of the Manley buildings, which allow for a maximum of six students in each one. These smaller spaces have proven to be more appropriate for certain types of studios where the research is more independent and focused, rather than studios where the collaborative experience is more critical.

In contrast to our existing studios, the new, large, open, and uninterrupted interior of the Murphy Studio Building presents a unique learning environment for the school. With a capacity of 156 people the school gained a space where exchange of ideas, sounds, voices, and collaborative experiences are engendered. We have learned that the ideal infrastructure for a school of architecture is one that includes a well-balanced variety of spaces for learning. There are studios and courses which are best served in smaller spaces and others for which the larger, open space of the Murphy Studio is ideal. The school can now accommodate small and mid-size teamwork, and large group collaborations as well as the more intimate and independent research activities.

The Murphy Design Studio interior, indefinite as it is, evolves time and time again, depending on the circumstances. In describing the qualities of the interior space of the Murphy Studio Building, I will begin with the floor plan and refer to Le Corbusier's conviction about plans as generators: "a plan calls for the most active imagination. It calls for the most severe discipline also. The plan is what determines everything; it is the decisive moment."[2] The building's open and modular plan with a centralized core of services has enabled the adaptability of the space to numerous and various circumstances, including the recent Covid-19 pandemic. The uninterrupted interior allowed us to accommodate for social distancing quite easily with ample circulation space all around. The high-bay, open interior has also generously accommodated our core design studio classes, while granting the School with infinite possibilities for space planning of the interior. We have produced over one hundred different layouts of the interior space. The interior is in constant evolution due to the flexible nature of the plan. Recently, we removed one modular floating office to double the central critique/review space in the center of the building. More recently, we removed a second modular floating office to address the health requirements for social distancing, allowing us to spread out the workstations accordingly. The demolition of these modular offices took only one day; reinstalling them if needed will take another day. In general, most of the furniture in the space can be disassembled, relocated, removed, and stored quite easily.

The selection process of all furniture, finishes, and accessories was a close col-

---

[2] *Corbusier, Le. Towards a New Architecture. Dover, 1986.*

laboration between the University's Design and Construction department and the School of Architecture Dean's office. The expertise of the University designers in outfitting institutional spaces and our own professional experience with interiors made what could have been a prolonged process a timely one. The interiors process should not be undermined; numerous samples of fabrics, furniture and materials were tested and mocked up in the space to optimize the selections. The exposed concrete (neutral) walls, the polished cement gray concrete floors, and the extensive glazed surfaces of the building provided an ideal background for studying color and light in the space. We were able to see what the fabrics and finishes would look like on cloudy days and bright sunny days quite easily. Although the criteria for the specification of all furniture and fixtures were primarily centered on design, durability, performance, and green certification, it became equally important to work with a color scheme that would animate the interior.

Some would argue that the interior is animated enough by sound. Being a very large room with a tall, open ceiling showcasing the exposed building's systems and grounded by the hard concrete floors, sound becomes a part of the sensorial experience of the space. Though there are mitigating factors such as the thick, felt red drapes surrounding the core bays, sound is a living presence. As students and faculty use the Murphy Studio more and more, the traveling sounds and voices have become more like white noise, allowing for greater focus. The understanding of sound in this interior has evolved from being slightly perturbing to necessary.

Another area where the building and its interior fulfill their roles as perfect places for pedagogy lies in the exposed type of construction utilized. Both the exterior of the Murphy Studio Building, with its exposed concrete formwork, and its interior offer an in-situ experience in building construction.

In particular, the interior has not only supported the design studio courses, but also the building technology classes where architecture students learn how architecture and building systems are integrated. They can easily understand the mechanical, electrical, and lighting layouts and systems because of the architect's decision to leave these exposed in the Murphy Studio. Additionally, it has facilitated the discussion on the challenges of designing system layouts in exposed ceilings rather than in enclosed ones. The intricacies of placing light fixtures, fire sprinklers, AC ducts and vents, and electrical and data drops are explicitly revealed. We even carried the "exposed" type of installation to the two floating offices in the building. These offices were built of a modular DIRTT panel wall system. During the installation we had an option to fully enclose the offices with walls made of colored enameled glass. We chose to leave one wall/panel of each of the floating offices in transparent glass to display how they are wired and powered from the ceiling.

In addition to transforming the physical, pedagogical, and social dimensions of the architecture school, the Murphy Studio Building has prompted a revalorization of the School's own existing buildings. It has been a catalyst for the renovation of our mid-century heritage buildings and for accelerating the conversations for future new infrastructure on the architecture campus.

The 1948 Marion Manley buildings, which represent the original school of architecture facilities, have been on a wish list for much needed renovation, repair and upgrading for decades. These buildings, merging shortly after WWII, are part of an "important grouping of modern college buildings [which] brought national and international attention to Florida. The University of Miami campus and its buildings designed by Robert Law Weed, Marion I. Manley, and Robert M. Little adapted the International Style to the tropics and were spotlighted in such publications as Architectural Forum, Progressive Architecture, L'architecture d'aujourd'hui, and National Geographic."[3] Soon after these Bauhaus-inspired buildings received historic designation in 2014, the School leadership worked tirelessly in ensuring that the much-needed renovations would follow. Almost immediately after the ribbon cutting ceremony of the new Murphy Studio in 2018, the School began working

[3] *Hochstim, J. Florida Modern: Residential Architecture 1945-1970. Rizzoli International Publications,2004.*

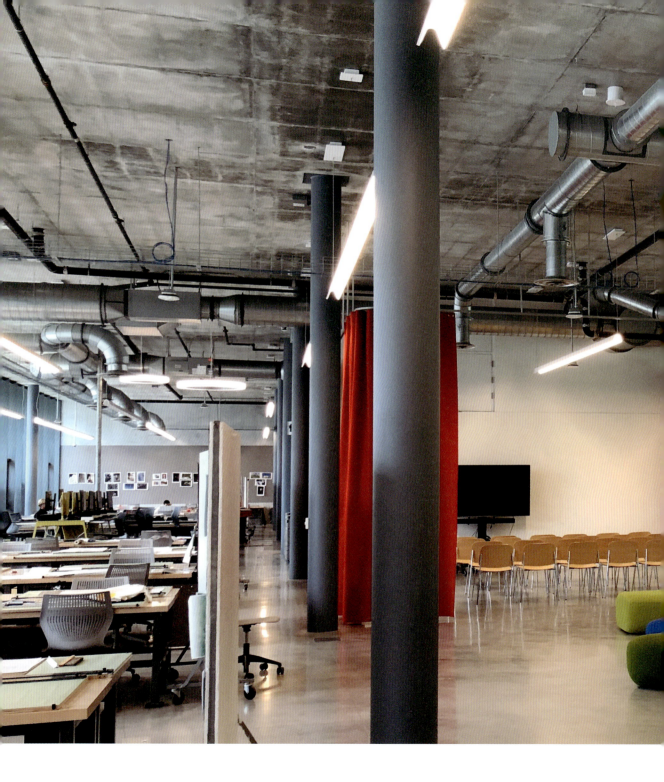

with the University's Design & Construction department and the City of Coral Gables on the replacement of the windows of the historic buildings. Because the windows occupy a very large surface area of these buildings, the renovation project has become more of a full façade redo, in which exterior walls have had to be rebuilt in order to replace structural members. We were able to complete phase two of the window renovation project just before the pandemic. These and more renovations have followed imbuing the architecture campus with a refreshed appearance and upgraded conditions that can be largely attributed to the Murphy Studio Building.

Today, in the face of a continuing pandemic that calls for the School to continue its mission in a safe and healthy environment, while accommodating an increasing enrollment base, the resilience of the Murphy Studio Building resonates and provokes discussions about future projects on the architecture campus.

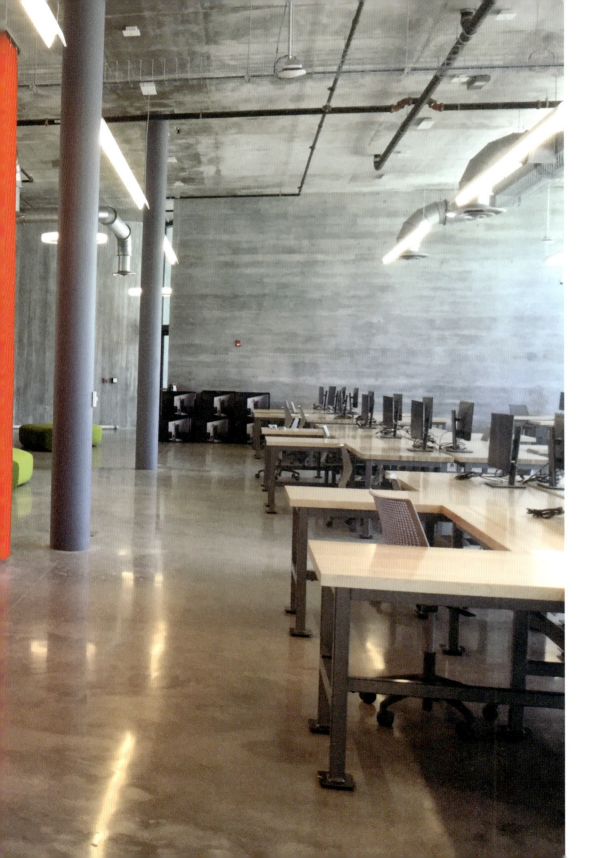

The Interiors

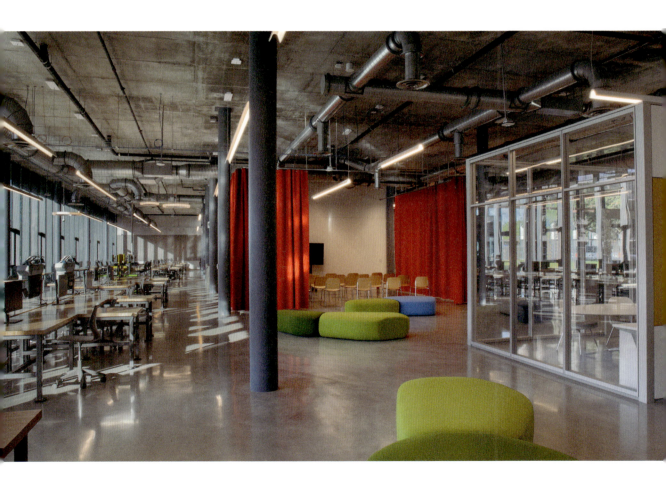

46 | The Interiors

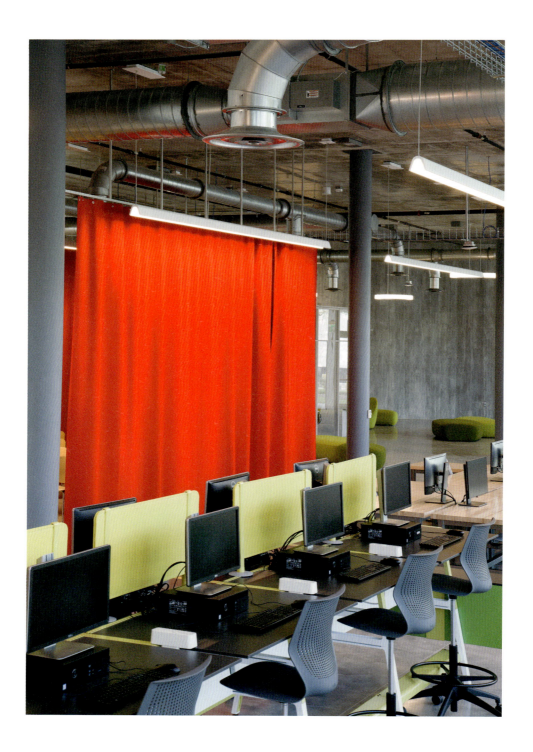

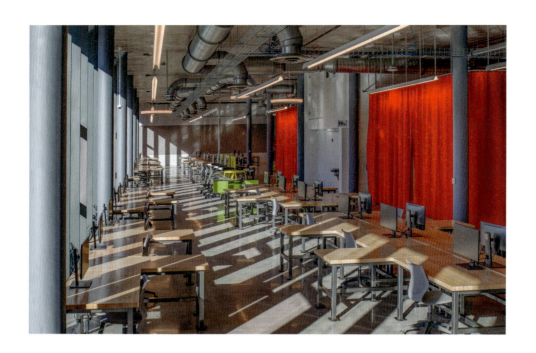

50 | The Interiors

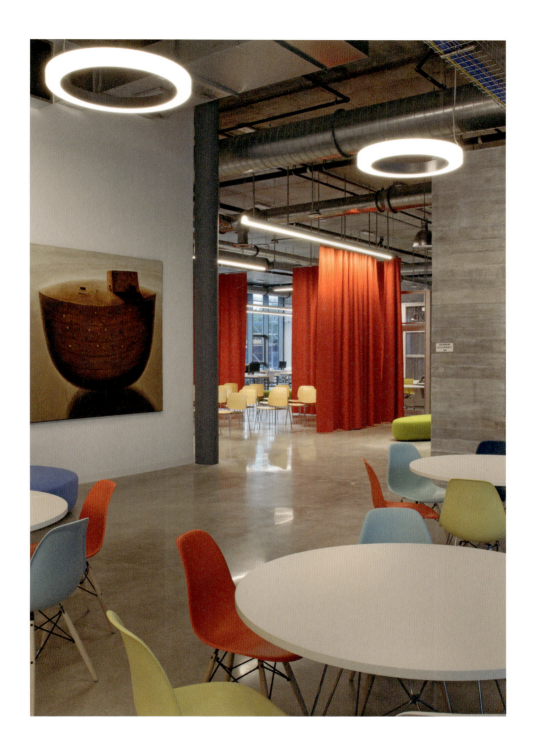

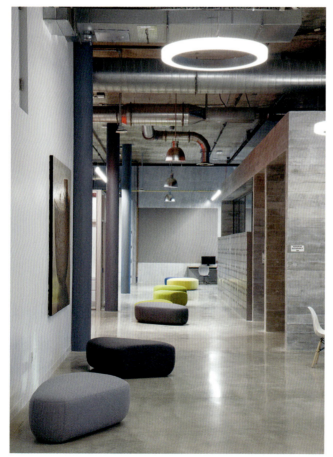

Conversation with the Architects:

Bernardo Fort-Brescia, Raymond Fort, Thomas Westberg & Carmen L. Guerrero | Arquitectonica International Office in Coconut Grove, FL | November 7, 2019

Interviewer:
Carmen L. Guerrero, Associate Dean of Strategic Initiatives & Physical Planning | University of Miami School of Architecture

You've worked very closely with two school of architecture deans in the production of this building, which has a direct impact on architectural pedagogy. What was it like to be the architect for other architects?

BFB
It's not just the deans, the faculty was giving opinions about how the school was to function as well. And there was debate whether we should continue the history of the "little cocoons in a little cubbyhole" sport, or whether to have a huge thing. When we started the design, the faculty gave opinions of what they were looking for.

RFB
The School of Architecture campus was defined by the mid-century bar buildings designed by Marion Manley, which give a lot of character to that part of the campus. They are converted residential dormitories, so they didn't necessarily serve the function as well as they could have for the school. The debate there was whether to continue that legacy or create something different. And actually, some of the early versions of the design of the new building were an interpretation of those bar buildings. Ultimately, it was elected to do more of a large studio space. It was something the school did not have. Dimensionally, we reference the width and length of those existing buildings in the final design. A typical structural bay in the new building measures 25 feet, which is the width of the existing bar buildings.

In comparison to the School's original, modest mid-century buildings, the new studio building, with its open plan, high bay volume and expressive form has drawn a lot of attention from the community, in particular from other university departments. It has positioned the School of Architecture as an innovative place for collaborative learning & working. How do you believe the Thomas P. Murphy Studio Building will impact the University of Miami campus?

RFB
Currently we are working on the new housing project next to the school, where we have provided learning environments within that, which makes it so advanced. I think sometimes it's difficult to know exactly what kind of impact the building will have on the community. One always hopes it's a positive one.

BFB
Do the other university departments use the building for their own purposes?

CG
I respond to many requests to use the studio building, from both internal and external cohorts. It is an attractive space for workshops, conferences, photo shoots, lectures, charrettes, and interdisciplinary collaborations. The community sees tremendous opportunities in the large open interior space and in the well protected exterior areas.

BFB
Really?

CG
Yes, really. The impact reaches beyond the School itself.

RFB
Wow.

Do you believe that the building's unique architectural character will influence future campus projects?

BFB
Well, I'd have to tell you, we get calls from clients who say, "I want one of those," as if you produce cookie cutter buildings. I got a call from the dean of the engineering school who asked what it would take for them to get one of those buildings, one just like that. Engineers think mass production, factory, and steel mills. Excuse me, on the same campus, just down the street? He meant the idea of the building, not an identical one. This is the only example that I have where somebody from another department references the studio building. It sounds like the demand is more common than what we thought. We didn't plan it as such, we would have never imagined it would have the demand of an event space.

RFB
I'm not sure there is a clear answer to know what the impact is going to be, but using the housing project we are building adjacent to the studio as an example, that building actually reacts to how people use the campus. The buildings are lifted on stilts, the pathways that were already there, that people were using, remained in

place. So, we weren't actually trying to change the circulation around the campus for the housing project. But for this, it was different, because it's a ground floor building. And actually, if you look at ateliers historically, a lot of them are located on ground floors, as well as on upper floors of buildings. Especially as relates to architects, designers, and the fashion industry, you find them occupying ground floor factory-type open spaces, where you can see straight into the studios. Our own offices here in Coconut Grove are on the ground floor. People in the neighborhood see what we are doing here for the most part, but not so intimately. They see some type of activity happening. So maybe one thing you could have expected is that being on the ground floor and on a university campus, people are typically walking or biking. It becomes a very pedestrian experience to come by this building. If you are on the road driving like in other parts of Miami, buildings are passed by pretty quickly, the experience is very different. The fact that you have this creative studio space that has 17-18 feet tall panels of glass, really invites the campus to look into it. The most you can hope for is that it inspires somebody else to think, "Well, maybe, I want people to see what I'm doing too." And it helps cross-pollinate those different disciplines across the campus.

RFB
The building has decentralized the School of Architecture campus. For as long as the school has existed, the heart and center has always been the courtyard along the lake. This courtyard is a bridge between the rest of the campus and the architecture school. With the addition of the Thomas P. Murphy Studio Building, the school's center has now shifted to another place, facilitating a path to the eastern boundary of the University of Miami campus.

How does the location of the studio building dovetail into the future master plan of the university?

TW
The Murphy building has its own gravity which impacts the dynamic of the space and master plan of the university.

BFB
In the master plan, the building has an important role; even the angle in which it is placed on the site. The angle mimics the actual angle of one of the Leon Krier wings, you can see the lineup. This was discussed with the university's facilities team, who thought we should adjust our angle to 90 degrees, but it was important for us to keep the angle, because it created two axes departing from the existing Krier tower. We were not being selfish. We were not looking for this building to be the focal point, because it's low slung. The walkway ends at the archway at the base of Krier's tower. The other walkway in the master plan ends on the other side with the tower, which is tall, you can see it from far away. In the latest version of the master plan, it is our intent to create an interdisciplinary campus for all the arts,

with architecture being one of them. In this future plan there are some art studios, there's a theater, there's performing arts, visual arts, and construction arts. They are all together around an open space in front of that big overhang where people are now congregating.

BFB
And in fact, that overhang will also serve as a stage for performances for an outdoor amphitheater that faces the long side of the building. And then behind it, there will be a theater and a museum, and other things surrounding, what will be, a central space that is bordered by the building itself. So that side of the building

embraces a triangular open space that focuses on the building.

With the addition of the Murphy Studio will the architecture precinct become a gateway to the campus, from the southeastern edge along Ponce de Leon Blvd?

BFB
It is more like a main square within the campus.

RFB
At the time that it was being planned, it was supposed to be a direct shot to the Metrorail from the studio building and it may still be in the future. So, it's more along this promenade.

BFB
Grab me a piece of paper, because I don't have a master plan here. Fundamentally, if the octagon is here, and the building is here, this takes you to the housing and we slide under the housing. This takes you to the station and there's another road and walkway that takes you to a pier into the lake.

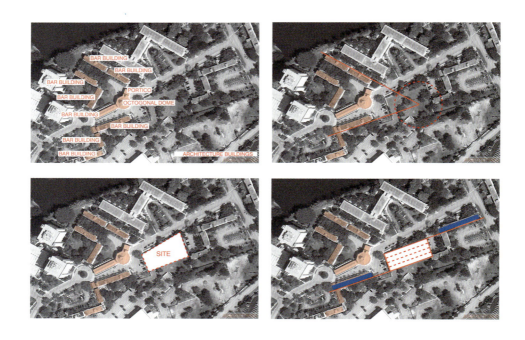

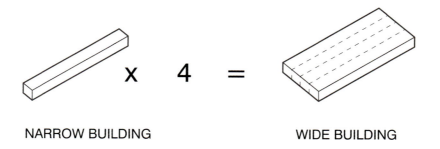

NARROW BUILDING × 4 = WIDE BUILDING

 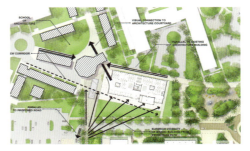

RFB
These are the existing midcentury bar buildings that inspired the four bars/bays of the new studio building.

BFB
The new building is an aggregation of four of the existing post-war buildings, So essentially, this is what's going on in the latest master plan; there's an art building here and there's another building here. This is an amphitheater, and this is the side of the studio building. This takes you to the lake and this ends in the tower. And the studio building is perfectly placed in that location. This is the housing that is creating that line, you see, so it's actually fitting in perfectly into the scheme of things. I believe this is the theater. This is the art studio. This is the Lowe museum here, and this is an amphitheater that everybody uses. And actually, the backdrop is that space, that porch.

So, the building is taking a much bigger role than was intended. And then of course, there's that little space here that was intended to relate to the Krier tower. If you look at the arch here, it focuses exactly on that space. In other words, if this is the box, the fact that this does this, is because the entrance lines up with the end wall. The fact that it's flat here, distorts itself to create that and make that little space. But this other space is for the amphitheater. So, it does have a role that it's more complex than just a building.

For this project the stakeholders are many; the School of Architecture community, the University's own Design and Construction department, the City of Coral Gables and the donors. What was the experience of working with all of them together?

BFB
It's a difficult question to answer because Coral Gables is a Mediterranean city. They have a strong preference for a Mediterranean architecture. While the University of Miami campus is very eclectic, it has a strong modernist approach to the architecture. Proposing a building that is modern may not be keeping with the city, but it's in sync with the campus in many ways, especially the School of Architecture campus, which is full of tropical modern elements such as eyebrows, operable windows, and exposed concrete.

TW
I think it has been dubbed as the first, all modern campus in the U.S.A.

ARQUITECTONICA
www.arquitectonica.com

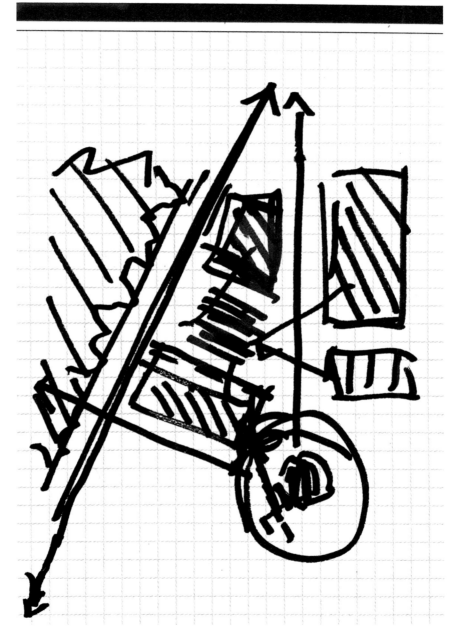

RFB

Yes, it is. So, as it relates to the City of Coral Gables Board of Architects, I think they understood that. We still had to guide them through how the project relates to its counterparts on campus. And I think, ultimately, they were happy with the result.

The City of Coral Gables is strongly committed to Mediterranean revival themes. Do you believe the city's perspective is shifting to embrace more modern and contemporary architecture?

TW

Yes, currently there is this "one size fits all" approach to aesthetic. I think the city's perspective can shift today because of the Thomas P. Murphy Studio Building's notoriety. If it was just a building that didn't get much attention, that was tucked away in the campus, then it wouldn't have much impact. Clearly, it has attracted much attention.

BFB

I think the city's starting to reconsider.

RFB

I was at the Board of Architects earlier this year in the hopes of getting a non-Mediterranean building approved and it was approved. It's a specific case, it was a renovation of an office building. But the interesting comment I received, which I remember distinctively, was that as long as the building held a strong enough character to one architectural style, they were okay with it. What they didn't want was a building that didn't have a style. This style just happened to be contemporary, so they felt that it was true to those principles, which they were trying to identify.

Do you believe the culture of the city is changing?

RFB

Yes. It's only just one project that I've been experiencing after the fact. But I think there is also a level of trust. At a certain point during the construction of the Murphy Studio Building, we actually had to take the drawings back to the Board of Architects a second time, because they were concerned about a change in the facades caused by a modification in the glass panels. When better technology comes out, you use it, right? That's how society starts to adapt to new things as they are introduced, like phones and so on and so forth. That's a strong example. To be able to use tall glass in a city like this, where we deal with tropical climate and storms, it can change the character of the city. Instead of having such solid buildings or buildings that require such heavy mullion usage, you can start to lighten them up. When you look at other cities that don't have our wind loads the glass is such a light object in the buildings. Here we have mullions that take can take up 15-20% of the actual surface area. This is something to consider.

BFB

On your question of style, we just submitted a project in the middle of Miracle Mile that is rather abstract, it is not Mediterranean and it's subdued in the composition, because the site is so small. The city thinks I am being nice in keeping it small, but I can't fit anything else on the site. We did not create a building with a crazy curve or anything; it is a rectangular building. It was approved, unanimously. It has no Mediterranean characteristics. The strongest advocate for Mediterranean in the city loves the Thomas P. Murphy Studio Building. He's the one who helped us get it approved. So, they're changing a little bit in their thinking. Maybe they realize this shift is necessary so that the whole city is not so uniformly Mediterranean. They are starting to shift a little bit from that.

How did the idea of the Thomas P. Murphy Studio Building project begin?

BFB

The beginning of this project starts with a call from Elizabeth Plater-Zyberk, former Dean of the School of Architecture. She asked me to help her out. She said the school was having difficulty recruiting students, because of the condition of the school's facilities. She underlined that UM students are often from well-to-do families, able to afford the expensive tuition. But that despite the student's desire to study there, when they toured the School of Architecture with their parents, and they look at the facilities, the parent's reaction is "I am spending all this money for that, how could these be the buildings?"

Parents don't understand that it is the faculty and not the space or building that attracts students to the Miami program. Parents have difficulty translating this, especially if it's an architecture school, which is about the physical world. Elizabeth said the school desired a new studio building and wanted to know how I could help get them organized to propose a showpiece building. So that was the beginning of the idea where we started working with a design, and I think we simply expropriated the site.

There was no site and we decided to do it where there was an empty space. It would have obviously fit in the existing courtyard but we didn't want to disrupt the courtyard and interrupt the view of the water. Where the new building sits was the most logical place to locate it. It fits snuggly into that corner and we felt it obstructed the least and that it could relate to the future walkways that the university expects to have going from point A to point B. We looked at the desired lines and it was logical to attach it to one of those walkways, the northern walkway. And then, I had to work on raising the money.

I had set aside some money and I told the University that it was for the only purpose of building this building. I told Lizz, and then I went out to look for donors, and I found Tom Murphy who was willing to donate the rest of what was needed to build the show-

piece building. In the meantime, the new dean, Rodolphe el-Khoury was appointed and successfully led the process to final construction. That's how it all started.

Now, obviously, I knew how much money I had raised. We needed to do a very simple building. This was not a multi-story building. Originally, we started with a building of less footprint and two stories to try to make it very compressed. But it was going to be too expensive, so we went all out and took more land. The University did not want single story buildings because they occupy a lot of space. It's not exactly a big building, but they wanted us to compress it, but there's a point when there's a minimum floor size. You can't do a little tower for a studio. We originally started with that because we could only use as much land. Often, I still hear it that we took too much land.

CG
Yes, we are known for being the smallest school on campus with the largest footprint.

BFB
Yes, exactly. I have heard that for a long time. While working on the master plan, I hear it all the time, the smallest school with the biggest footprint. Our lot coverage, so to speak, is huge. But, I totally disagree by the way, because the other schools have big green areas in front. When you include their proportional share of the green, we are not the biggest one. There are multi-story buildings next to a big green, so it's not fair that they are calculating only the building. They must include the proportional share of the green space as well. Their claim is not necessarily true. The next campus project we are working on is the high bay building not far from

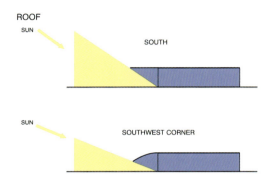

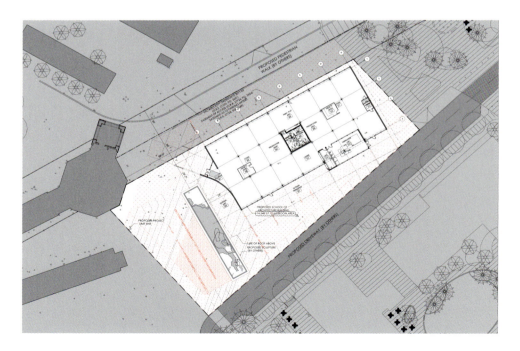

76 | Conversation with the Architects

the Murphy Studio Building, the triangular one. The University told us here again that we are occupying too much land for the size of the building. But in the artistic world, that's how it happens. It's very different from the law school or the business school who do not work in open, studio type spaces.

The artistic disciplines thrive in open studio spaces, that's how they are everywhere in the world. I think we are winning the battle on this one. The reality is that if you raise the money, it is very difficult for a school and/or university to deny the construction of a building.

Was it unusual for you as the architect of a project to also be involved with the fundraising of the same?

BFB
It's unheard of. But I knew that was the only way it would happen. The school wasn't going to come up with the money. And in fact, they never came up with a penny. In other projects, the school or university contributes, in this case, I had to seek 100% of the money. This was a struggle for me because raising money is a difficult and at times, embarrassing job. Normally I do not ask for money, I hate it.

Fundraising is a profession, right? It's not what we do as architects. In this case, I had some degree of authority to raise the money, since I had made a contribution for the new building. Being an architect and former faculty member of the school, I had a story to tell when I went out to fundraise. Particularly since I'm an architect, it's different than if someone else, like someone from the development office is asking for the money. Donors react to me in a different manner, they take the ask in a different way. I was more a part of the narrative.

Going back to the building itself, the idea was to create a real architecture studio. Frankly, I don't think we expected it to be a building that would be used by others.

CG
We don't say yes to every request to use the space. While we try to accommodate, we steer away from disrupting classes and studio work. Fortunately, there are center bays in the building that we use for reviews which can be isolated from the rest of the studio by drawing the drapes together. These centrally located spaces lend themselves well, for other uses without disrupting the studio environment. It's a perfect place for meetings, workshops, charrettes, and events.

How is the shape of the Murphy studio building a "natural" one, as I have heard you describe it?

BFB
Can you bring me a book and a piece of paper so that I can discuss the shape of the roof? I don't know if you're aware of how organic and natural the shape of the roof is.

RFB
This is looking from where the current site is, in the existing building. Here are the Marion Manley buildings which I understand are going through window replacement.

CG
Yes, we just completed phase two of the window replacement project.

RFB
They made them operable now, right?

CG
Yes.

RFB
Good. The operable windows in the new studio building were a contentious topic with the facilities department, very contentious. Back to the campus drawing, this is the only piece that is not dimensionally correct, but it serves as a node. I would argue that this building re-centers the whole area.

BFB
Actually, Krier's octagon was previously at the edge of the architecture precinct and now, with the new studio building in place, it's in the middle.

RFB
Right.

CG
That's right. We now have multiple centers in the architecture precinct.

RFB
This was an important view, through that port, and through that archway. And, if we take these two lines, this building kind of sits at that moment, where this portion of the campus terminates at the school. So that kind of defined the site. We made up the parameters. There is a road, a building and a parking lot. The two bar buildings on either side serve as this dimensional guide. They wanted a wide building, but we wanted to make sure it was respecting the dimensions of those narrow existing Marion Manley buildings. We placed four of them together, for the south light

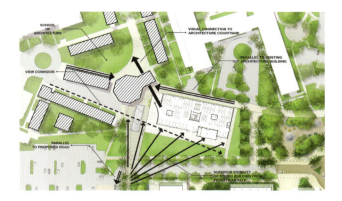

and penetrating pathway. This piece is added on to address the existing buildings, the portico, the plaza, outdoor workspaces, and upper jury area. We organized the plan by placing the restrooms and jury walls in the center of the space. Then you have the café space, and the offices which can float wherever. I don't even think the freestanding office pavilions are in this location anymore.

BFB
The intent was that they could be anywhere.

CG
We did relocate one of them so that we could gain additional space for one of the central jury bays. And more recently, we have moved it again, closer to the curved wall in order to gain a full bay for a larger jury or simultaneous multiple juries.

BFB
One of our ideas was that those little office pavilions would be temporary installations, designed by faculty and/or students, like follies in the middle of the space, demountable and not part of the architecture, as in a bazaar.

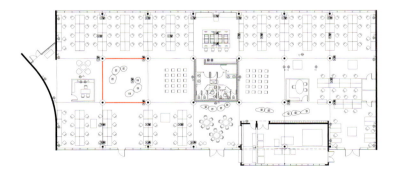

CG
Disassembly is actually quite easy, it only takes a half day.

RFB
That's amazing. So, in essence, there's this internal corridor of the building and it originally was supposed to terminate in a little garage door, so that you can bring things in from that side, drive a truck up, but that was closed up. The fabrication lab expanded to have a little cafe on the edge, so things changed. The roof evolves as you walk from one end of the building to the other, it's a very organic curve. And the curve, in a way, mimics the form of somebody curling their hand over an eyebrow to block the sun from one angle.

BFB
Because that's the southwest corner, the corner blocks the sun.

RFB
If the sun's coming from this side you use your left hand, right? Blocking that, and use your right hand for the other side.

BFB
The roof dips only in one direction. The roof takes on a natural dip as if it were a piece of paper floating over a box. This shows that the angle is not arbitrary. It's the actual stress over concrete that actually creates the dip in the roof. We calculated that's exactly how it would have deflected. Additionally, the dip allows for protection from the strong southwestern sun, by blocking it.

RFB
As for the board-form concrete, the direction in which the wood planks were arranged was intentional. In order to arrange the planks of wood horizontally along the curved wall, you would have to bend the wood for the form, or steam box it. By orienting the planks vertically on the curved wall of the building, we eliminated the difficulty of bending the formwork. So, the orthogonal, straight walls of the buildings run the concrete forms horizontally and the curved wall runs the forms vertically, along the portico.

BFB
Ultimately, the location of the building was sited at 90 degrees to one of the facades of Krier's octagon of the nearby Jorge M. Pérez Architecture Center, and it lines up with the wing where you have Glasgow Hall and it follows the road and it is coincidental with the actual. The Murphy Studio Building is in a perfect location in regards to the future master plan. Once the campus master plan is built out, there will be more density, plazas and walkways on the southeast of the studio building, facilitating a more legible connection between the School of Architecture precinct and the metro station, the water and new quads on the campus.

Why was concrete chosen as the primary building material?

BFB
Concrete is the material that is used in Florida, as opposed to steel. It was interesting to show the students how we build here. In this building you see the concrete in the walls, in the ceiling and in the floors. It is not concealed here.

RFB
This was interesting to build, because as you can see, the contractor needed to understand how to put these curves together; it's such an organic curve. This is a long curve, it's not a straight line. And this is also a curve and in plan view, you actually see, the roof plane is being pulled down by the curve.

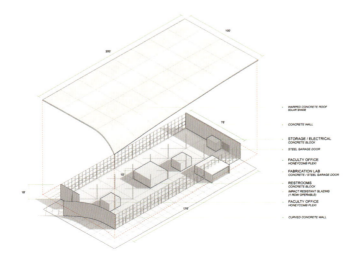

There's this triangle in that little triangle too. But then the control points in this direction were spaced at every two and a half feet, and then it spread five feet where the curve wasn't as dramatic. So, the way that Coastal Construction built it was literally by measuring from grade up, and then hammering a piece of white wood to mimic the bend and then slowly laying out flat strips.

BFB
The roof was a real feat for Coastal as well, they're very proud that they were able to build it.

Do you consider the partnership with Coastal Construction a perfect fit of architect and contractor?

BFB
Yes definitely, most contractors would have objected. They would have pleaded for changing the roof design. Together with Coastal Construction, we created a true learning environment for the architecture students. There's all kinds of construction systems and types that the students can observe in the building, such as metal columns, a concrete roof, exposed concrete walls, glass walls, fixed windows and operable windows. There are operable windows inserted into the larger fixed windows. The mechanical ductwork and electrical lines are all exposed. So, you can look around and see how a building is actually built. It's like an encyclopedia building. The raw nature of the building facilitates an understanding of how the building is built. Usually you don't see any of this in a building because it is concealed. It is a true in-situ experience.

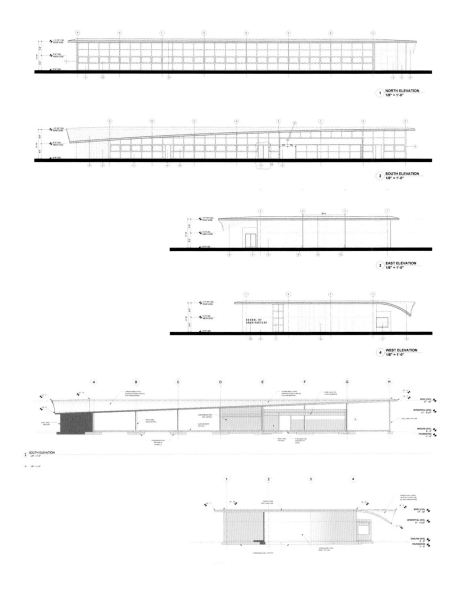

RFB
See, here is the drawing showing every number we plugged in denoting the heights for the curved roof. We could have sent the contractor a 3D model, but they really needed this drawing with the numbers in order to be precise.

BFB
It's an interesting drawing.

The Exterior

111

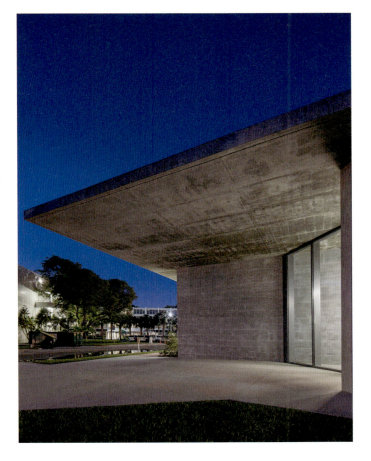

Conversation with the Builder:

Thomas C. Murphy, Sean M. Murphy, Patrick E. Murphy, Nick Duke, Jason Anderson, Coastal Construction & Carmen L. Guerrero | Coconut Grove, Florida | November 12, 2019

Interviewer:
Carmen L. Guerrero, Associate Dean of Strategic Initiatives & Physical Planning | University of Miami School of Architecture

What was your father's motivation in building this iconic project for the School of Architecture at the University of Miami?

TCM
My father attended a couple of classes at UM. He is a very proud UM alum in his own sense of the word. I think it was in the late 80s when Ron Fraser was around and they were trying to complete the baseball stadium project. He got a call from Ron Stone who asked him to help him finish the baseball stadium. Right?

PEM
No. It was the Athletic Director at the time who called him, Sam Jankovich.

TCM
Ah, that's right. So, he asked if he could come out and help them get the stadium done. Through a process of phone calls and getting people to volunteer to donate materials and/or labor he was able to get someone to do the painting, someone to get the drywall, someone else to donate the framing, and in summary, was able to pull a team together to complete the stadium. He made some donations of his own as well. Since then, over the years, we've been donors to the University of Miami.

PEM
To explain why we got involved in the project, it is worth it to offer some more history. Bernardo Fort-Brescia took our dad to lunch, to talk to him about this and made an ask for the new building. And at that moment, I think it was clear to my dad that number one, he loves the University of Miami. Secondly, he cherishes his relationship with Bernardo, therefore, who made the ask was important. But the bigger, more macro, thought was, everything that we do as builders begins with architects. And so yes, we have some architectural interests internally. The relationship between architects and general contractors is critical. So, by funding a building for an architectural school, is a great way to set an example for the industry about that connection between architects

and GCs. And it all kind of came together very nicely. It was a selfless way in a sense for him to look at this project.

Was the stadium project your dad's first campus project?

TCM
That I am aware of, yes.

Was the Murphy Studio Building his second project, or were there others in between?

TCM
There were others. The Thomas P. Murphy Design Studio Building was the second donated project on the campus. There was also another building, a smaller one on the School of Architecture campus, that we were donors for. You can see it from the Ponce de Leon side of the architecture campus. It's a four-column structure with wood louvers. It was right around the time when we were building the President's house in 2012.

CG
Yes, that is our beloved B.E. & W.R. Miller BuildLab

TCM
Yes, we provided a donation at that time of which part of it was intended for this little building. Our relationship with the School of Architecture is not new.

PEM
We know Lizz Plater-Zyberk and several of the professors at the school. We are always interacting with them in one way or another, whether it be in the community or at the school.

119

Tom Jr., the first time we met some years ago, you expressed your passion for architecture, and that you once thought of studying architecture. Were you inspired by your father's interest in construction?

TCM
It's interesting, I think I got it from my father through birth. I have always had affection for architecture. Growing up I knew my dad was a builder. And when I went to college at the University of Florida, I ended up getting into the School of Architecture. My family, as far as I was concerned, was not interested in architecture. And so, I guess, I actually studied architecture on my own, on what I thought was my own engagement. And through the years, I have come to learn that my dad is a frustrated architect, as well.

PEM
Dad got into construction, in many ways, because of his dad; because of our grandfather, who was a painter and who worked with our dad side by side in the same office for decades. Our grandfather had ideas, but he was more of a painter, who had worked with his hands, more of a hands-on guy. Grandad got dad interested in construction early on as he grew up. They were best friends, they did everything together, similar to how close we all are. When grandad passed it was very tough on all of us, especially on dad. The founding of Coastal was the best way Dad could honor the legacy of his father.

Do Erin and Sean share the family's affinity for design and building?

TCM
Sean is definitely an artist.

PEM
Yeah, all through college he was drawing cartoons. Sean was interested in building construction. But he has an artistic sensibility.

SMM
Yes! I have always enjoyed creativity, design, drawing and the entire construction process.

Erin, what is your formal background?

PEM
I did finance and accounting at UM. I did accounting for a little while, and then politics for a little while, and then back to construction.

CG
Erin, I remember meeting with you on site. You were always on site and very

helpful during construction.

What was it like working on campus and building a structure that is so different than the other buildings on our campus and from others in the City of Coral Gables?

ND

Just off the top of my head, the initial challenge was in finding who was going to actually do the work. We are dealing with a workforce that's not necessarily skilled or talented down here in Miami. This made the selection of the subcontractor to do the formwork very, very important for the project. We were sensitive to being in the heart of the campus and having pedestrian traffic around the job. But the main thing in the back of our heads, all the time, was that Tom Jr. could pop in any day, so the site needed to be perfect. We ran constant inspections of the quality of the work and thought through from the very beginning stages of what the finished product would be and worked backwards from there. So, on an exposed concrete building, you're not hiding any of your mistakes. If your electrical boxes are in the wrong place, and don't function for the end user, it's never going to look good if you try to move it. So, we really had to think about, from the foundation, to reckon the wall around the foundation. What will the finished building look like?

And as you know, sometimes the plans aren't as developed to that extent to get to the end. So, there was a lot of coordination. I think what made it really easy was that all parties involved from the university, the architect, and Coastal, were all in on making sure that it was done right. It was the least adversarial job ever. Everybody bought into this idea that this was going to be something special. Whatever it takes to make that happen, that's where we're going.

What did you all learn about a process that involved an institution such as the University of Miami, a school of architecture and the city of Coral Gables?

JA
There was a difference of opinion on windows. So, you had the architects that wanted the windows a certain way. And then you had a client that wanted the windows in a completely different way. And it was interesting to see how you had basically, two people coming from the design side, on what they wanted and then talking through how they were going to ultimately decide on who was going to win that debate. The university got the say on it in the end, but really, it was a bit of a compromise from what they initially wanted. It had to do with operable windows versus fixed windows. When you add the operable element, you add a horizontal member. Arquitectonica wanted full glass. I think what ended up happening was out of six bays of glass, there were two operables for every six. I can't remember the breakdown anymore, we increased the amount of mullions, the width got lessened, but we didn't have a horizontal break as frequently.

[Bernardo Fort-Brescia coincidentally approaches the table]

TCM
Bernardo! Hello! We're sitting here talking about the Murphy Studio Building. And this is our interview for the book. We were just talking about the window design.

CG
What a coincidence!

PEM
This project was like building a home. All the stakeholders are so happy with the end product. I've not heard a negative thing about that. And the hundreds of people I've talked to about the building, everyone loves the building. I've never heard anyone say, oh my gosh, it should've been a Mediterranean style building or it should have been bigger or smaller, to me it seems to have somehow met everyone's expectations.

CG
Because of the nature of the immersive design studio classes that take place in the building, it is like a home. Our students work there throughout the day and sometimes don't leave when they have deadlines. This is not a classroom that operates during business hours only, nor one that students are disengaged with. Students keep their belongings at their designated workspaces. Their stations are their own office spaces.

TCM
Archi-torture, I remember those days... I completed up to design three. So, I went through my design one, two and started design three. And I remember I spent 48 nights awake, 48 all-nighters in the first 16 weeks of school. My professor told us that if we had time for any other class other than his, we would fail. I'll never forget that.

CG
Surely those semesters of design nurtured your appreciation and understanding of architecture.

TCM
Oh my goodness, completely. I studied architecture in high school where I enrolled in two or three design classes. Then I got accepted into the University of Florida and absolutely loved it. When I sit there and I listen to Bernardo talk about it, I get excited.

During the process of construction and the day to day logistics, did any of you sit back and think about how such a building would transform the school, university and the city?

PEM
There has been a pretty low barometer for architectural prowess on campus. In the day to day you have to talk about the construction of it, you're talking about the quality control in order to make sure that what you're building is the finished product. And you can't hide anything so there can't be any mistakes.

ND
It's the old saying, "go slow to go fast" though, right? So, you have to catch yourself where the builders were incentivized to look for efficiencies and speed things up. But whenever you're doing something like this you are fighting against your own natural tendencies. You have to really think about things and triple check everything.

SMM
We had a different understanding as a family. To us, we weren't just being asked to

build a building, but we were asked to be involved with it. So, when we're looking at it from that perspective, or going through the design early on, and working with the architects, the design team, and to complete the drawings, we had a better understanding of what the program was, what the vision was, because we were involved in it. Many times, we were just given the set of plans and asked would you please go build this? So, we would go build it. This was different, we understood we were there from the beginning, getting involved very early on, right up front, as Arquitectonica was coming up with the basic concept of taking that concept to a new set of plans, and understanding what Bernardo's vision was and how to help create that.

How did being the builder and donor impact the final product?

SMM
Literally, we were sitting at both sides of the table. It gave us a sense of ownership and pride. We knew the cost of any design changes and we knew the vision well and appreciated that certain things had to be done and could not be eliminated.

How do you think this type of building with an open plan, high space and exposed systems will impact teaching and learning?

PEM
It will enable a new, more modern way of learning, of working, and collaborating. The trend in work environments is to take down walls a lot. We see that in the WeWork shared office space concept. It's all open with no barriers. I think it is really attractive and contemporary. And I think that's evidenced by the growing number of students applying to the school right now. Growth has been exponential. This is a clear indication that students want to study at the U-SoA.

ND
No detail was too small. Nothing was unimportant to consider in our conversations about this building.

Did you expect the building to resonate with the community as it has, with consistent interest in utilizing its interior and exterior spaces for a variety of activities?

TCM
I think we all saw it as something cutting edge. I think we could see the relationship that it would have to the outside. I mean walking inside the building, inside being outside, the height of the clear glass. When you are inside the building you still feel connected to the landscape, to the environment, to the street, and to the great big oak tree out the back. There was a lot of discussion early on about the open space and how the school was going to react to the noise in the space. And it's interesting to hear now how that noise is actually part of the life and character of the building.

The new studio building proves that new construction in the City of Coral Gables does not have to follow a Mediterranean Revival language to get approved. Do you think that this will change the local perception amongst those in the construction industry?

PEM
Probably important is the context. It's within a campus, the middle of a campus. Yes, it's the Gables, but it's inside the campus and not so visible from main streets. I don't think you're gonna see that on Le Jeune or on Ponce. So, you know, I don't know, maybe I'm wrong.

TCM
Maybe it's a starting point, at least for the campus to be able to relate to something else other than the traditional heritage of the city.

The studio building uniquely offers in situ contact with materials and building systems; an important lesson for architecture students. Is this your first experience in building with exposed concrete and exposed building systems?

JA
I worked on a project called Neo Vertika, which is a 36-story condominium, where it's loft style, so it has exposed concrete, exposed AC ducts and fire sprinkler pipes. We were familiar with building in this manner.

PEM
And that was an intended component of the design, right? I remember that it was very much intentional to be able to show the students that the more that can be exposed, the better. But it's that much more effort for Jason to keep an eye on quality control; that everything is straight and installed right, like clean pipes and all that.

CG
It's a great lesson for students because common thinking is that it's much easier and inexpensive to build in this manner because it is more "raw." But, actually this type of building requires more coordination, quality control, and special fixtures.

SMM
There's a lot more coordination up front, a lot more.

JA
Another thing to think about when you're building like that, is that the subcontractors doing the concrete, mechanical, or electrical systems are used to having their work covered by drywall or stucco. So, they are not shooting for a beautifully finished product. They aren't used to actually producing the finished product, the one that is visible and seen by everybody. They know that their work typically gets covered

up and because of this, it does not have to look perfect; it's not exposed to the world the way that it is in the studio building. This type of work is not something that most subcontractors are used to doing.

What does Tom Murphy Jr. think of the new studio building?

PEM
What does dad think of it? He is extremely proud of the building. Every time he hears a new report about how the numbers are skyrocketing for enrollment, that to him is the ultimate achievement. Of course, he cares about how it looks, but the fact that it's helping the university and the school in advancing their goals and attracting global talent is like the apex. I don't believe he ever imagined the impact this building has had.

TCM
I don't think he ever even had that thought.

PEM
It's made our dad so proud that, I think he's thinking about how we can continue to stay involved in the school and the university. The relationships we have built with this project are important.

TCM
Bernardo might have had that idea when proposing the building, that it would be transformational for the school and the university.

What are the most valuable lessons learned from your father?

TCM
My dad is a workaholic with great passion for his work. All his partners are aware of this. He grew up in a family business. We work just as hard and are passionate about what we do.

PEM
Growing up, I lived in 21 different houses, condo and apartments. We moved at least once a year, and so I had to be very understanding of the turmoil involved by always moving. We would move in to our dream house and then six months later, he sold it and we would move again.

JA
I'm kind of excited. I know that Tommy and Sean had built buildings and homes for their father. And I never had done that. I avoided that role for a long time. And this was an opportunity where I drew the short straw and got to build the building. Now

I'm excited to pass that on to Erin, who gets to be involved in his next endeavors in building a house.

Hearing all of your collective experiences with design, we (the school) are fortunate to have worked with a builder so intrinsically connected to our discipline. What advantages did this give you on the job?

JA
I think it's important that for an architect to really get their design implemented to the fullest extent, it's important to have a builder that has the same forward thinkingness; a builder that knows what the architect wants and is looking at it from the architectural perspective, as opposed to just building exactly what's on paper and let the outcome be whatever turns out.

CG
This project seems to have been a perfect match of architect, builder and client.

TCM
Yes, I agree. Everyone involved seemed to have a unified vision about the building and end result. We knew what it was going to be design wise, what the budget was and then we had to merge them. We were successful in doing so.

JA
The other thing that I think maybe you can speak to this also, but everyone that we worked with at the university was fantastic. I mean, probably I can't think of a project where there was a client that we were working with, where they were so knowledgeable, competent, professional, and really had a focus on doing things the right way and treating people professionally. And how to move things forward and make decisions in a timely manner. I mean, it was just, it was a really refreshing experience, at least for me personally.

I thought that they were fantastic to work with. We spent a lot of time with Gary Tarbe, and we thought that he was just great.

CG
Well, you know that Gary went to architecture school. He's an architect.

JA
He was just an excellent person to work with because, one, he knew how the university operated. He would know the things that would maybe cause a little bit of an issue. Whether it be a neighbor down the street that complains about the concrete trucks at six in the morning. He knew all the little, the little tricks of the trade, so to speak, of working on campus and would get out in front of that truck with us early and just a real pleasure to work with.

Do you think you will do more university related projects, campus projects?

TCM
Hopefully.

The Drawings

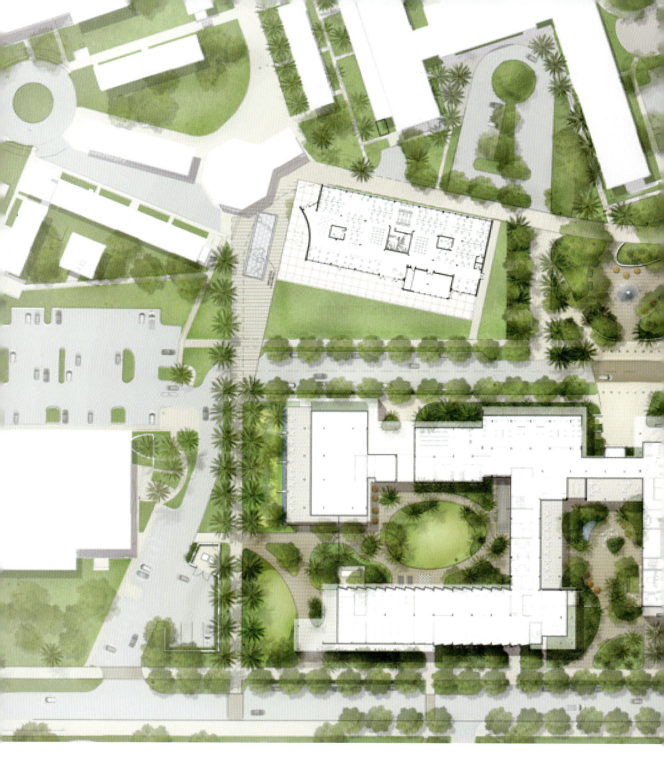

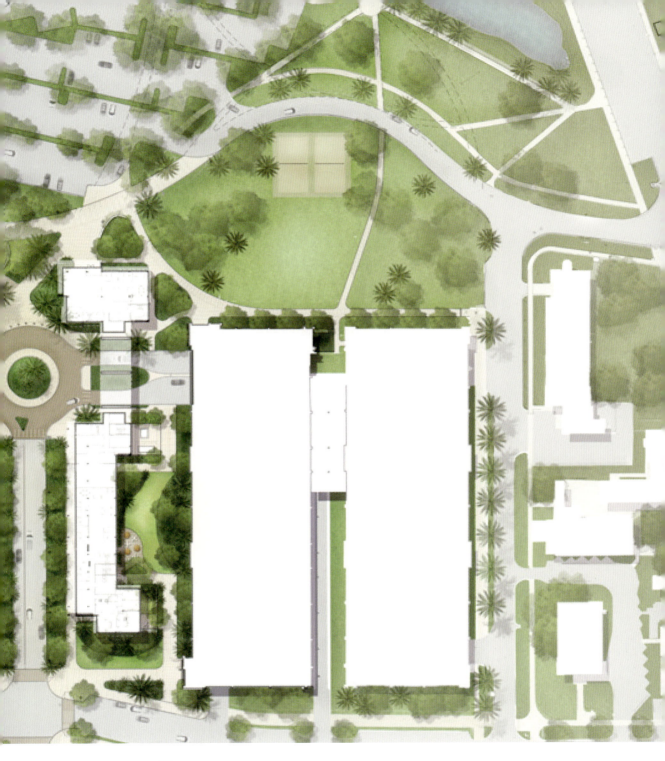

Site Plan

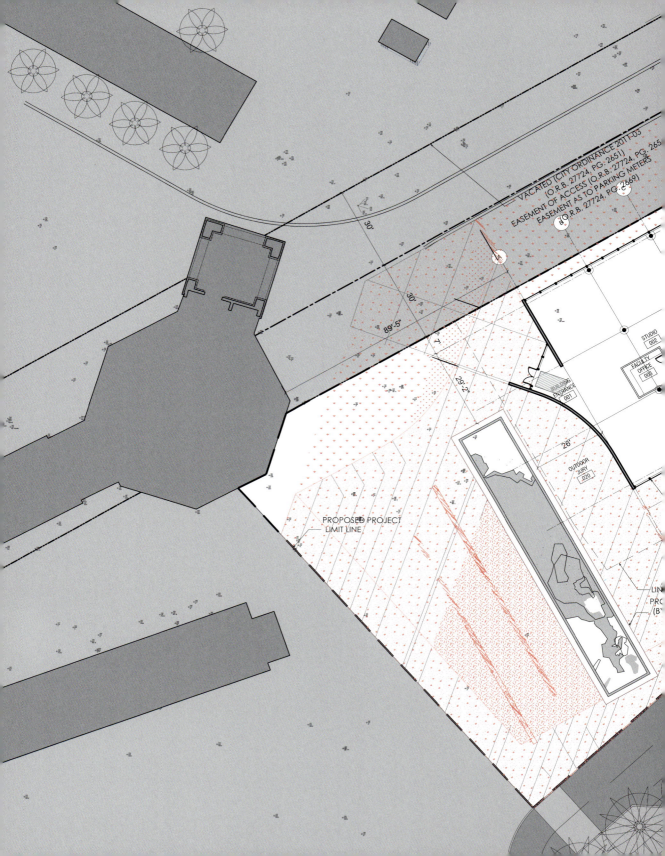

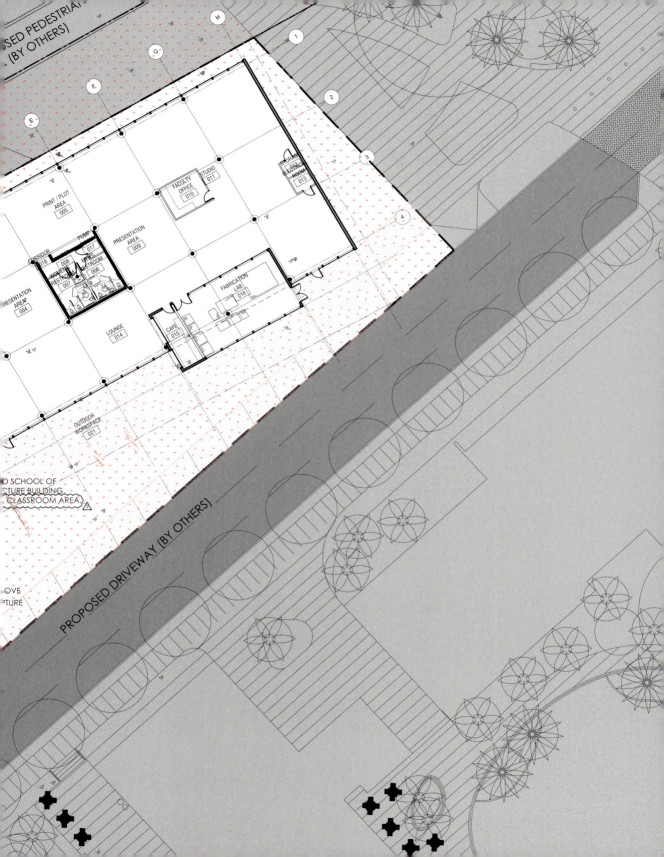

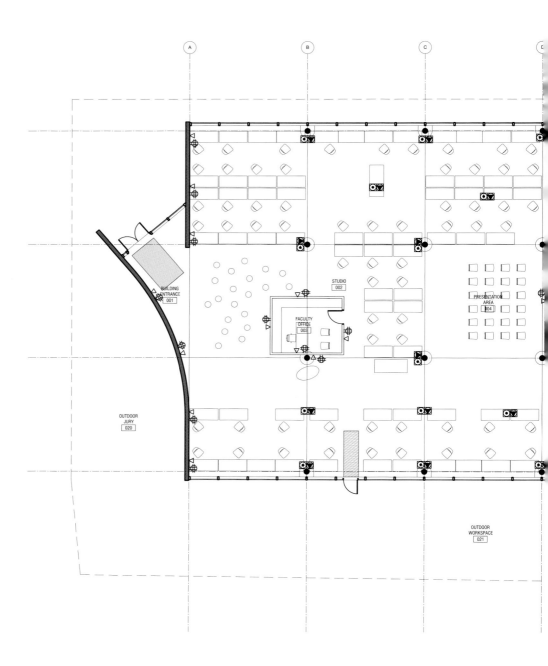

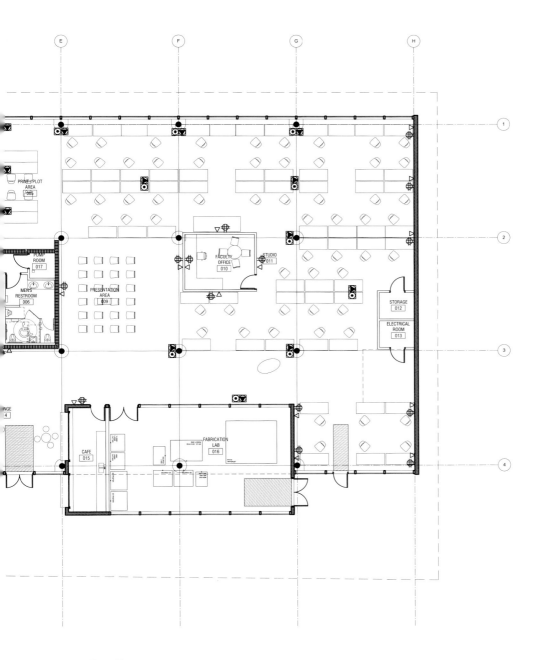

Floor Plan

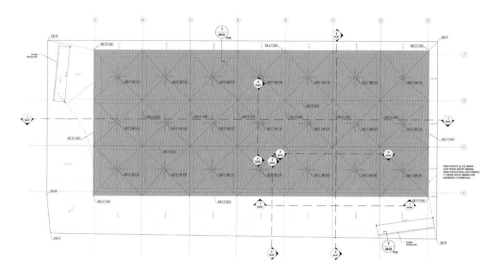

Roof Plan | 1/8" = 1'-0"

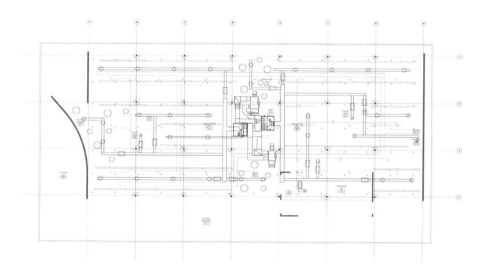

Reflected Ceiling Plan | 1/8" = 1'-0"

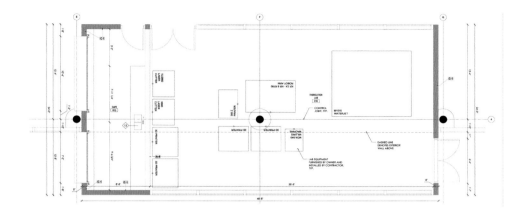

Enlarged Floor Plan | 3/8" = 1'-0"

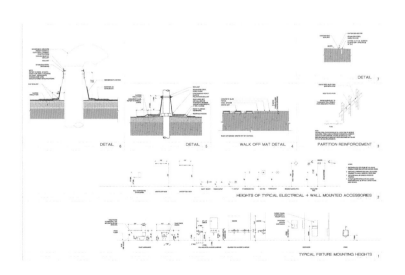

Americans with Disabilities Act Details

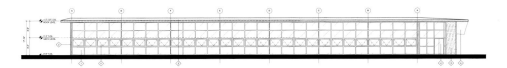

North Elevation | 1/8"= 1'-0"

Section | 1/8"= 1'-0"

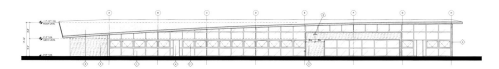

South Elevation | 1/8"= 1'-0"

Legend

1 | Glazing system
2 | Cast in place concrete wall with wood formwork texture white wash finish. Vertical or horizontal pattern as shown on elevations
3 | Concrete roof
4 | Glass door
5 | Hollow metal door

6 | Concrete celing with white wash finish
7 | Roll up aluminum counter shutter door
8 | Emergency overflow scupper
9 | 3/4" Reveal
10 | Sign formed in concrete, 12"h letters, font tbs by architect
11 | Awning window, typical.

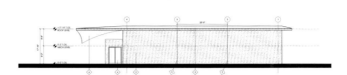

East Elevation | 1/8" = 1'-0"

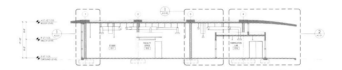

Section | 1/8" = 1'-0"

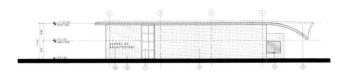

West Elevation | 1/8" = 1'-0"

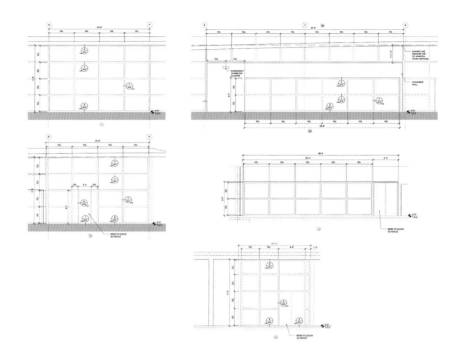

Window Schedule | 1/4"= 1'-0"

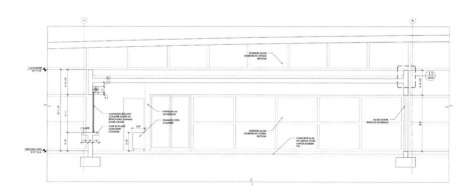

Wall Section | 3/8"= 1'-0"

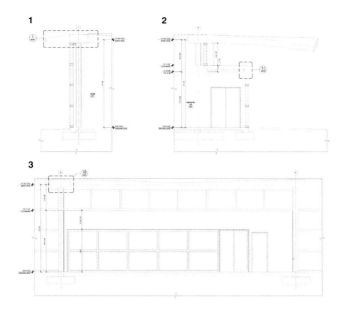

1 | 2 | 3 | Wall Section | 3/8" = 1'-0"

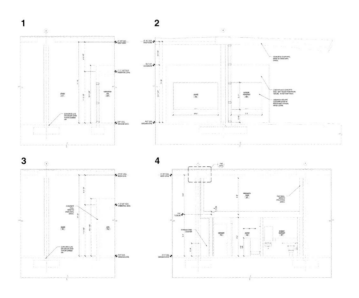

1 | 2 | 3 | 4 | Wall Section | 3/8" = 1'-0"

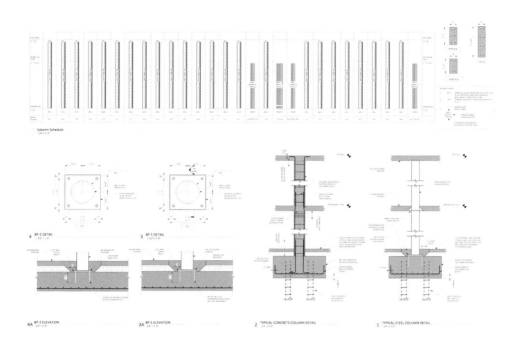

Column Schedule & Details

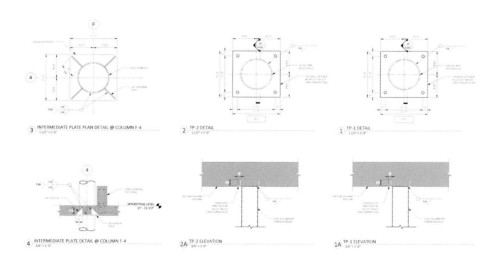

Column Details

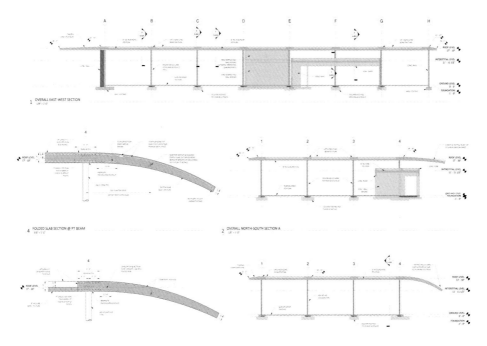

Sections & Details

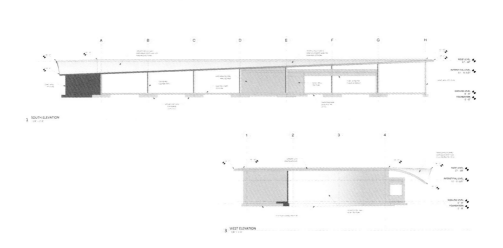

Elevations

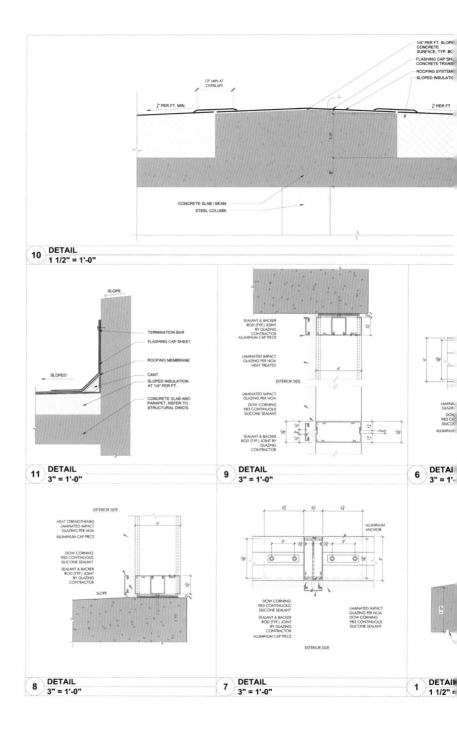

Details

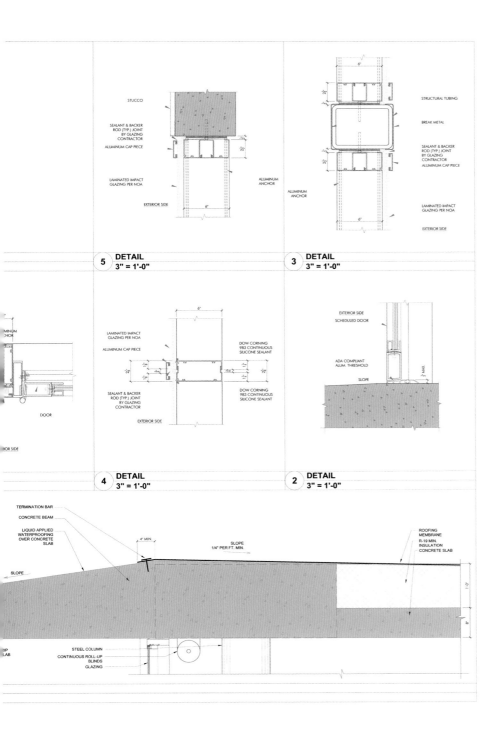

Conversation with the Curtain-Wall Manufacturer:

Jose Daes, Carmen L. Guerrero & Emily Nelms | May 14, 2020

Interviewer:
Carmen L. Guerrero, Associate Dean of Strategic Initiatives & Physical Planning | University of Miami School of Architecture

It's a great pleasure to meet you, Mr. Daes. Your company provided one of the most favored aspects of the new studio building, the glazing. Could you tell us about yourself and how you became involved with glass?

JMD

In college I pursued industrial engineering at BU in Boston. After 3 years I found that I wasn't learning anything that I liked so I told my dad that I didn't want to go to school anymore. I became a college dropout. I went back to Colombia and I started working in textiles with my father. I made some good money those days, in my 20s. Then the importation of textiles was prohibited in Colombia and I went out of that business. I came to the US where I opened some high-end Italian clothing stores in Miami: one in Miracle Mile, one in Dadeland and one in Bal Harbor. At 24 years old I was fitting the most important people in Miami, the best lawyers, the richest people, but then after 5 years, I realized this business could not grow any further. In 1983 I had invested in a solar water heaters venture. It was very small, but we transformed it to window making in 1988. And in 1988 we sold $60,000 in windows and we grew to $10 plus million by 1993. Then we decided to open Tecnoglass, which is the company that actually makes the glass and we entered the US market in 1995. We found a really good buyer; his name was Raul Casares. He was the owner of R.C. Aluminum Industries. He introduced us to the market. At the beginning he was buying only glass from us, but after a couple of years we began to make the windows for him. That's how we got into the US market.

In 2008 we opened our own aluminum extrusion plant. In 2013 we went public because our company was not recognized in the US and people didn't trust us, because we were from Colombia. In 2014, we bought our own sputter coater plant to make Low-E glass. It was a big investment for us, circa $50 million. Then, more recently, we invested with Saint-Gobain for a float plant. We now have a float plant in Bogotá and there is where we source our clear glass. We are going to build a second float plant in Barranquilla next to our factory which will position us as the only fully vertically integrated company in the whole world.

What is a float plant?

JMD
It's an industrial production where raw sand and a few chemicals are mixed, then heated above 1500 degrees centigrade to melt them. It's called a float plant because the glass floats over a pool of tin, like oil floats on top of water.

Where are your projects located around the world? Are they more concentrated in Latin America?

JMD
We have projects in Colombia, Peru, Bolivia, Chile, Argentina, and in Panama. We have projects all over the Caribbean Basin, especially the islands. However, 90% of our sales are in the US. We are in Florida, Texas, California, Illinois, Massachusetts, New York, Maryland, Washington and, Tennessee. And now we're expanding to North and South Carolina and Georgia. We are all over. We're doing a lot of work.

One of the most interesting aspects of the Murphy Studio Building is that is has the largest single-pane impact-resistant window in South Florida? Is that correct?

JMD
That is correct.

I came on board when the project was in its beginning stages of construction, the window design had already been finalized. I know that there had been a significant window revision. Can you give an account of what led to this change order?

JMD
This is what happened. The architects produced a window design based on what they thought could be done at the time. The design included a lot of transom horizontal aluminum profiles. The horizontals were more than double of what they are now. And when I saw that, I thought it was absurd to let it happen in a building that was going to be so beautiful. Having so many horizontal mullions would have hurt the overall glazing design. So, I called Bernardo Fort-Brescia, the architect, who is a dear friend and a very talented man, I mean he's unbelievable! I asked him, "why do you want to kill the project by putting in so many interruptions to the clean glass facade?" I mean, that looks like a jail. It doesn't look like a nice studio. So, we rebuilt the sample and it made a huge difference. I'm not completely happy with this final design, because they still installed too many operable windows. In my opinion, the operable windows should have only been placed at the ends of the facades and that's it. Then the rest should have been clean panes of glass.

This is a controversial topic at the School of Architecture. We have never been able to open the windows of our studios in the existing mid-century modern buildings. Most of them have been bolted closed to avoid stress on the mechanical systems caused by the extreme temperature differentials when we opened them.

JMD
Then you should change those windows also!

CG
Fortunately, we are in the midst of doing so.

JMD
Do you know what's the most important feature of the studio building? When you move through the studio, you don't see any distortion through the three big panes of glass even though they are all tempered. This is almost an impossible feat for any other manufacturer. I mean, go out to the Miami airport and you will see a lot of distortion when you walk through the space. Our glass has the best quality of any manufacturer in the Americas.

Without divulging too many of your secrets, why is that so? Is it because you invest more in higher quality materials?

JMD
It has to do with a few things. Number one, the tempering furnaces that we have are the best and most advanced in technology. Number two, when we started selling in the US in '95, a lot of people rejected our glass because they checked it with magnifying lenses, instead of doing it the proper way, because we were from Colombia. So, they thought it had lower quality.

Because of that hurdle, we worked very hard on our quality. Our company slogan is the "Power of Quality," because we overcame the paradigm of the quality issue. We don't do random selection of quality, we do quality assurance in five different areas for every piece of glass. And number three, we have the best working environment. Our employees make 15% to 60% more money than the average employee in Colombia and have many benefits. We pay for their children's education, whether it's school, high school, or university. And that's why they are fond of the work, because of the way we treat them. And after 10 years with the company, we improve their housing, or we give them the down payment to buy a new one, or pay their existing debt. We have many programs for them, because the only way to have people fully dedicated to the work and quality like the owners, is to reward them accordingly. We share 5% of our profits with all of our employees. Everything starts with relationships and how you treat people.

Despite your wish to have seen less operable windows in the elevation designs for the Murphy studio building what is your overall impression of the finished product?

JMD
I cannot sell what I don't like. I like to be proud of what I do. I am very oriented to dressing well, looking well, eating well, and enjoying my life. I love to see that the results of whatever I'm selling makes everybody else happy. In this case, everyone is happy: the Murphys, the University, the School of Architecture community.

You have had previous experience in working with the University of Miami on campus projects, correct?

JMD
Yes, we do a lot of the housing projects. The general contractors working on the campus such as Coastal, Bosch, etc. always call us to supply the windows.

Has your strong conviction about quality and design ever forced you to walk away from certain projects?

JMD
I found out too late in life that it is better to walk away from a job, than to lose money. It's better not to stay if the situation is not right. We walk away a lot, especially, when people do not have integrity. And that's why we do work with companies such as Coastal Construction, Related, and Jorge M. Pérez.

> "Our company slogan is the 'Power of Quality,' because we overcame the quality issue."

Tell us more about new the technologies that allow for more extensive glazing in tropical climates such as ours, where too much glass is not always desired due to heat gain.

JMD
If you look at the early ages of construction, like the pyramids, or castles, they were 99% solid and closed with very few openings to protect themselves from the weather, and the outside. Today, people want to be integrated with the outside. That is the effect we got with the studio, because of all of the glazed surfaces, once you are inside the building you feel like you are protected from the exterior

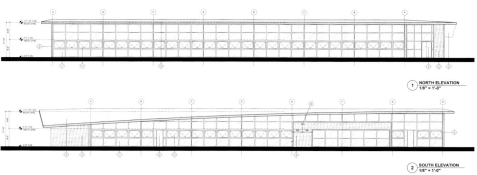

160 | Conversation with the Curtain-Wall Manufacturer

landscape while also being integrated with it. The future developments lie in electrochromic glass, which is glass that reacts to the sun by becoming opaque. When the sun shines on the glass, the glass will darken itself and will not let the heat in. With this technology you will need less air conditioning.

Is this electrochromic glass already in the market?

JMD
We are currently working on a real solution, which is unbelievable. We are planning on having it in the market perhaps by next year. A lot of companies are working on making glass to function like a solar panel which absorbs energy and passes it through to the building. You need less energy, because you produce it. The cost is so high that not many people produce it in America, unlike Europe which is more eco-friendly. They are years ahead on everything that has to do with glass in comparison to the US.

Who are your competitors?

JMD
We have a few competitors in the residential market. Our prices are a little more competitive. Three years ago, we saw a commercial slowdown so we entered the residential market in 2018, 2019 and 2020 and now we are producing so much that it's unreal. Residential glass now represents about 30% of what we sell and it's going to continue to rise next year. We have shorter lead times than most competitors.

What are the lessons learned from working on a project that brought together an institution, a school of architecture, city officials, a builder and a vendor such as Tecnoglass?

JMD
What I can say about this specific project is that when everybody is in line to do something, everybody's expertise adds value to the process and the end result comes out perfectly. When there is conflict between parties regarding costs and/or design and you have to compromise, the results are usually not optimal. That is the reason that when people complain to me about glass not being efficient enough in their building, I remind them that someone in the project actually made that choice. In the case of the Murphy Studio Building everybody wanted to make the best of it, from the designers to the owners, the donors and the builder. This is something I value tremendously.

Conversation with the University of Miami Project Manager:

Gary Tarbe | May 18, 2020

Interviewer:
Carmen L. Guerrero, Associate Dean of Strategic Initiatives & Physical Planning assisted by Emily Nelms | University of Miami School of Architecture

Gary, you are an alum of the University of Miami School of Architecture and were involved with the construction of the Murphy Studio Building as the University's project manager. How do you believe your training brought more value to your role in this project?

Gary Tarbe
Yes, I studied at the University of Miami, but when I was there, it wasn't a school. It was part of the College of Engineering at the time. We were taking full engineering courses from the School of Engineering, such as structures, concrete, strength materials, and statics. We had some great design professors. At that time the master's program was being developed by Jan Hochstim, Paul Buisson, Aristides J. Millas, all really great instructors at the time. It was a great education.

I think that having a project manager with an architectural background helps maintain the integrity of the design. Project managers with similar backgrounds can understand how architects think. We can make educated decisions on project modifications that do not compromise the core aesthetic and architectural intentions.

As the Senior Project Manager for the Design and Construction department at the University of Miami, what are your responsibilities?

GT
The Design and Construction department oversees the planning, design, construction and occupancy of all construction projects on campus. Project managers are assigned to a project prior to job commencement.

Sometimes PMs shift off occasionally, from one project to another, but that's just a matter of workload at the time. We take it from concept to construction to completion. We are responsible for hiring the architect, whether it is through a design competition or an RFP process. We work with them and the client on the program development. Our client is the university personnel or department; usually it's group of different folks that contribute to the project. We work with them all the way through the programming and schematic phases of design and through the permitting process and the bidding and negotiation phases. It's a soup to nuts.

It's a PM's responsibility to make sure all the players play together nicely, and make sure it's fair, and that everyone is treated well. We often refer to ourselves as "owner's rep," rather than project manager. In this case I represented the university. As far as the dean of the School of Architecture and the board, and everyone else, they're relying on us to pay close attention to the job. It was my responsibility to relay information about design, budget, schedule, and changes back to the owner.

Also, adding to the team of players involved, both the architecture firm and the general contractor assign their own project managers to the job.

What was it like working with Coastal Construction in comparison to other contractors you've worked with in the past?

GT
Working with Coastal was a very good experience, to be honest. I found them to be very good to work with, very professional. They had a great field team, project manager and superintendent. They did a very good job. They are up in the higher echelons of their industry. Paperwork was very important; the RFI's, change orders and submittals were all done very professionally and for as straight forward of building it is, it was not an easy building.

Coastal is a homegrown company which grew very rapidly. I've been around a while and remember that they started out doing high-end residential construction. They had celebrity clients. Now they build large-scale projects and are comparable to other companies such as Skanska and Moss.

From the beginning this particular project was a collaborative effort involving the School of Architecture, Mr. Tom Murphy and Arquitectonica as well. It was known that Coastal Construction would build the job.

From your perspective what was Coastal's most valuable skill in this project?

GT
They were they resourceful in finding solutions for problems that did not compromise the aesthetics of the building. The superintendent is really responsible for the day to day operations and for the nuts and bolts. Coastal's superintendent

Thomas P. Murphy
Design Studio Building

was excellent. He was always thinking outside the box, and from a logistics standpoint, which is always a very big item on construction projects.

How has the physical environment of University of Miami and the School of Architecture transformed since you were a student there?

As a student, I really wasn't aware of how things worked. I think it was much different back then. Obviously, the university was much smaller, fewer buildings, and a whole lot less landscaping. To be honest, I can't even really remember a project underway while I was there from 1973-78. The real expansion of the facilities didn't happen until later, when everything was pretty much built out. When I talk to my co-workers, the Design and Construction department hadn't even been developed until just a few years before I got there, about 15 to 20 years ago, when expansion and new building really took off.

When I was there the School of Architecture was in the engineering building. Basically, we all worked out of our dorm rooms. And we didn't have studios, which was fun in a way. They housed us all on one floor of Pearson Hall, which was high living at the time. So, all the doors were open, everyone's music playing, everybody's wandering the halls, looking and talking, and it was a really great community. That's really the way an architectural firm kind of works. These are qualities we find in the new Murphy Studio Building which is wide open, with lots of natural light, all of which adds to the ambience and is inspirational. The space is shared by over 100 students in there at one time, day and night with people coming in and out. There's always movement in and around this building.

How is the Murphy Studio Building positioned within the master plan vision of the campus?

GT
It's right in the heart of things. As it turns out, the School of Architecture has its own master plan. I looked at it several times and noticed they're planning on expanding as much as possible. The Student Activity Center or the Donna E. Shalala Student Center was actually the first I was assigned when I started working at UM. The student center sits on the lake and shifted the center of campus from Stanford Drive over to Dickinson/Miller. The spine of the campus now is through the new housing project, which I also worked on. The core of the University campus is now much closer to the School of Architecture. Previously, people probably wouldn't even know the School Architecture was there, because it was off the main circulation route, but now it has a very central position. Through the years, the campus has shifted a lot as a result of new construction.

What existed on the site where the Murphy Studio Building now sits?

GT
There were some of the 1940s military barracks, similar to the older buildings of the School of Architecture campus, which had been converted into student housing and classrooms. There was an agreement between the University and the city of Coral Gables to keep those in the architecture precinct for historic preservation purposes. The rest of them were demolished to make space for new buildings.

You can tell the barracks are architecturally significant, but because they're 1940s utilitarian buildings, they were built quickly and inexpensively. There was also a parking lot and outdoor volleyball court on the site. It really wasn't a well-defined or organized area. It was utilitarian, it worked. Taking them down really opened up that portion of the campus a great deal and created opportunities to better connect the architecture school with the main campus.

What were the challenges in building an exposed concrete structure, both inside and out with exposed ceilings and systems?

GT
Well, the success of such building boils down to finish work. You can't just pour a wall hastily and rely on drywall to cover and conceal all the imperfections.

It was desired to have walls illustrating the formwork in a particular manner. In this case, we used very large form panels and lined them with actual wood, and then we poured the full height of the walls. We poured about 20 lineal feet at a time. You can see where the seams are. The walls are at least 12 inch thick. When you pour something that tall, the pressure at the bottom is tremendous. So, to avoid blow outs, the tie backs and whalers, on the outside of the forms, had to hold the material. They were all steel forms. It's not something you do every day.

Another interesting thing about the Murphy building process is that when we removed all the wood lining and planks, we donated the materials to the BuildLab, so that students and faculty could use it in the future. It was reused, repurposed after we used it in the formwork.

In an exposed system building, everything has to be coordinated. The duct work is not regular duct work, it's got to be spiral, because it looks better and it can't be externally heavily insulated. It's all internal. Those are some of the reasons it gets to be a more expensive way of building. Common thinking is that if it's all exposed, it's got to be cheaper. Well, not really, if you want it to look nice, you can't rely on traditional and regular mechanical or electrical work. We installed a very nice cable tray all the way around the exposed ceiling so that the free wires for the data look organized. You have to make sure your light fixtures aren't over-

lapping with the ductwork. Coordination of everything in the ceiling is facilitated by the use of CAD and Revit which allow you to see how it all lays out two and three dimensionally.

There is nothing like this building on the campus. The Cox Science Center is an older campus example of exposed concrete construction. For Arquitectonica, exposed concrete is one of their signature materials.

How did you ensure the connection between pours is clean and seamless?

GT
Everything gets cleaned up. Usually, you overlap one form with the other a little bit, with the previous pour. All the rebars must be continuous throughout. Any horizontal rebar should be continuous through to the end of the next pour. We didn't buy all new wood for all of the pours. Wood gets reused as well as the forms. You pour a wall here, and a wall here, you strip them, move the forms. When you look at the plan, there's really not that much concrete wall area. There's just the two short end walls of the rectangle, with one of them being curved. And then, you've got the roof. The roof required all new wood and formwork, because it was exposed and had to have a specific finish. For this we used form board which has an almost plastic laminate feel to it. And then, there's the famous dip of the roof.

It seems that there is rational approach to the design of the Murphy building that is in perfect tension with its organically sloped or "dipped" roof. What were the challenges of achieving this roof curvature?

GT
The roof is a real credit to the form workers. It was a top-quality framing job. Using modern methods and software such as Revit models, provided a lot of information, a lot of data points that were critical in achieving the curvature. Building the curve out of plywood and two by fours was not the easiest thing in the world. We didn't use a big Styrofoam form or anything like that, which is sometimes what you might do on smaller curves. They form workers just built it and bent it all the way down with the help of data from the digital software.

How is the dip of the roof supported formed and supported?

GT
Good question. We had to build a base of scaffold, up to the highest point. Then we used that as a base to build off of. We had to build at least eight feet or more of height to make up in certain areas. The whole roof is a post-tensioned structure with cables throughout including PT beams. The roof actually gradually thickens from the thin edge you see at the outside to approx. 18" thick, and you don't see it architecturally. If you get an aerial, you will see the crisscross pattern of the beams.

One of the best stories of the project had to do with the building of this curved roof. Hurricane Irma hit Miami while we were in the middle of construction. After the storm, all the project managers got called to walk through all the ongoing campus projects to check for storm damage. As I returned to the office from being at the Murphy building, I ran into my boss who told me that we had just received a call about the collapse of the Murphy roof. I told him I had just been there and that everything was fine. We had just poured the roof right before the storm. So, we walked back together and looked at the site and there was nothing there, no damage. When we dug a bit further into the nature of the call, we learned the caller thought that the roof had collapsed because of the drop in the curvature.

The modifications to the glazing design represented significant revision to the original design. Could you tell us about the logistics involved with this revision?

GT
Well, there's a story about the glass. We started with one system, but Dean el-Khoury wanted something else. He wanted very tall and continuous glass, but we just didn't think it could be done. Ultimately, with Tecnoglass we achieved a great result.

Because of the hurricane codes all glazing systems have to have what's called an NOA, or a notice of acceptance. That means that it's a system built out of bits and pieces, and there are certain spans and wind pressures that it can withstand. The new height of the glass is 17 or 18 feet tall at the high point, and there weren't any systems that had an NOA for this height. We had been working with 10 feet or 12 feet glass which would withstand the load. Tecnoglass wound up saying, "Yeah, we got a system and, you know, we can do it."

They managed to get it approved, structurally, which was good. The mullions have steel inside and are at least 12 inches deep. The glass is very heavy and thick. We did run into a little problem with the City of Coral Gables Board of Architects because of the revision to the exterior elevation, but the university architect, Juan Rodriguez-Vela managed to get that resolved. The board agreed the new design looked good. In the end, Dean el-Khoury's vision led to a great decision.

The Experience

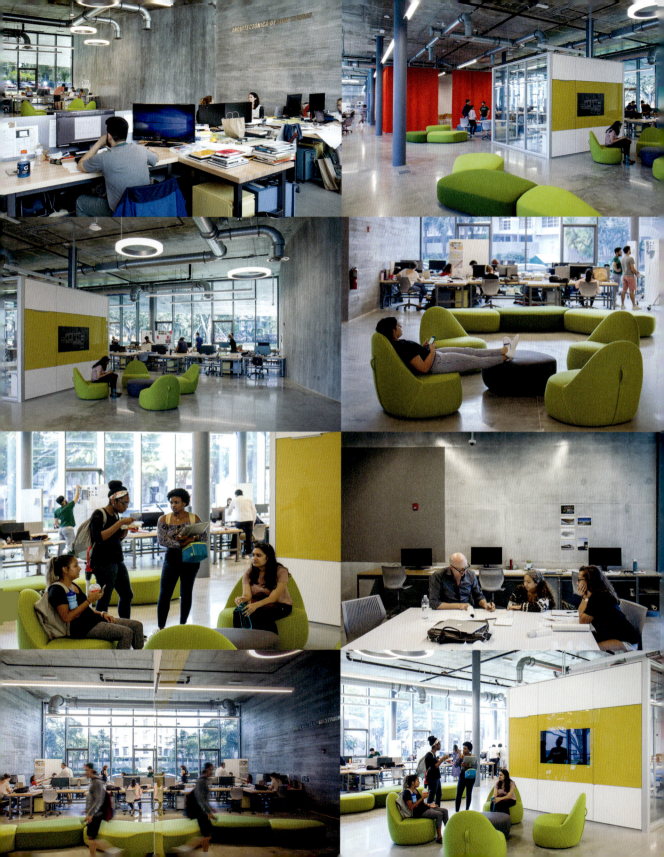

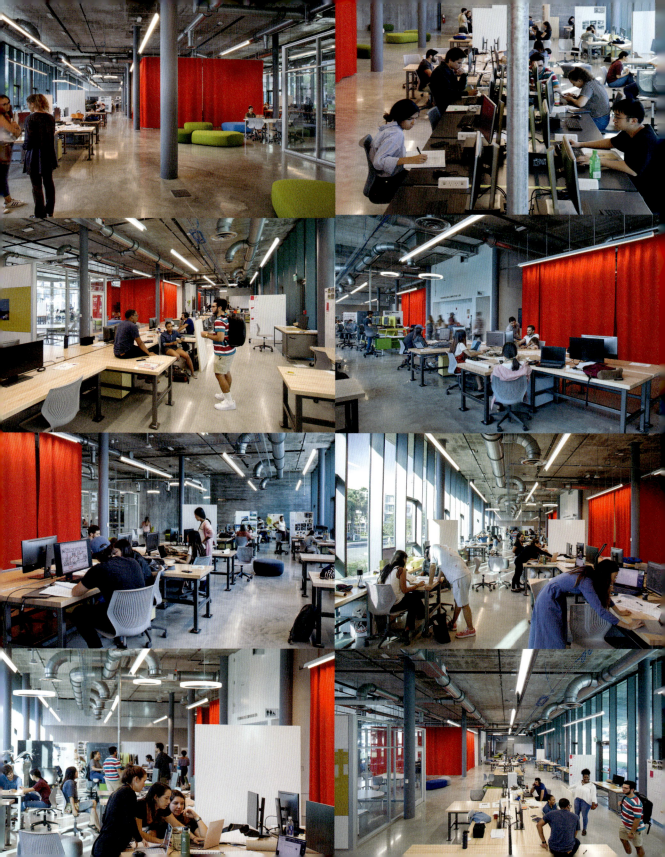

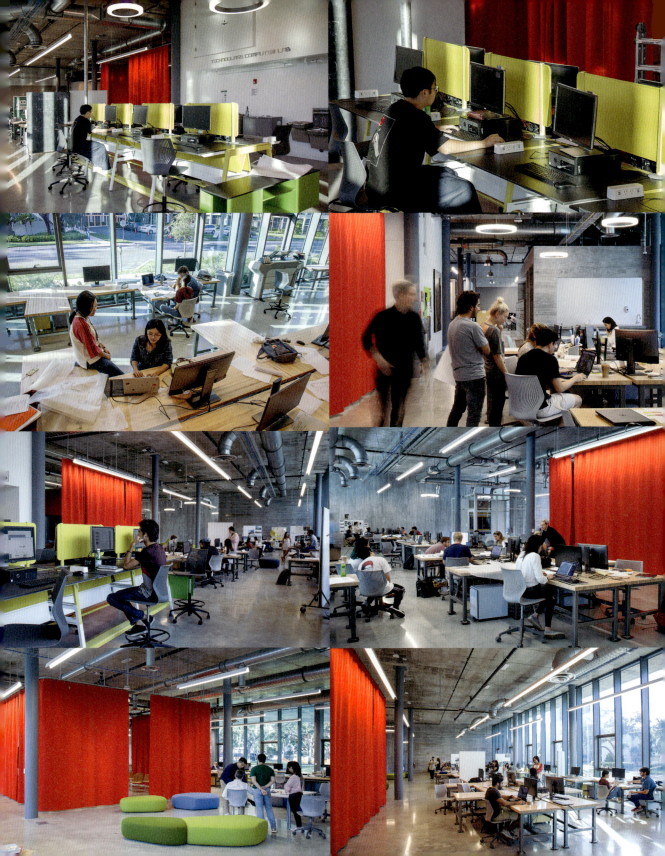

Building Credits

Manufacturers:
DIRTT Environmental Solutions, Versteel

Architect of Record:
Sherri Gutierrez

Civil: VSN

Landscape Architect:
ArquitectonicaGEO

Geotechnical Engineer:
NV5

Interior Architecture:
ArquitectonicaINTERIORS

Interior Design:
Maggie Binmelis & Juan Rodriguez Vela, UM Design & Construction Carmen L. Guerrero, School of Architecture

General Contractor:
Coastal Construction Group

Construction Manager:
Coastal Construction Group

Structural:
GMG

Sustainability:
SUMAC

Partners In Charge Of Design:
Bernardo Fort Brescia,
Laurinda Spear

Project Director:
Sherri Gutierrez

Project Manager:
Rafael Guissarri

Project Designer:
Raymond Fort

Acoustical:
Shen Milsom & Wilke

MEP/FP:
Stantec

Specifications:
Arquitectonica

Survey:
Atkins

Client:
Facilities Planning & WConstruction

MEP:
Stantec

Fire Protection:
Stantec

City:
Coral Gables

Country:
United States

Book Credits

Book Layout by Florencia Damilano.
Art Direction by Oscar Riera Ojeda.
Copy Editing by Kit Maude & Michael W. Phillips Jr.

Photography Credits

Peter Leifer & Cheryl Stieffel of Miami in Focus, Inc.: 2, 34, 37, 40, 44, 51, 52, 90-92, 100, 102, 104, 106, 108, 176, 178 (top left), 179, 182 (top left), 183 (top right and left), 184, 188, 190.
Robin Hill of Robin Hill Photography: Cover, 4, 13, 36, 38, 41, 42, 44(below), 45-50, 54, 55, 73 (below), 93-98, 110-114, 178 (top right), 180-183.
Carmen L. Guerrero: 28, 63, 130.

Carmen L. Guerrero & Kalil Mella: 18, 29, 73 (top), 84, 86, 120, 122, 131.
Arquitectonica: 60, 64, 70, 75, 76 (top), 82,83, 172 (top), 172 (below)
Gary Tarbe: 82 (top), 119, 124, 125, 156, 169.
Tom C. Murphy: 123, 126, 133, 166.
Jose Daes: 160 (top)
Ivonne de la Paz: 22, 25, 30, 170, 171.

OSCAR RIERA OJEDA
PUBLISHERS

Copyright © 2021 by Oscar Riera Ojeda Publishers Limited
ISBN 978-1-946226-53-2
Published by Oscar Riera Ojeda Publishers Limited
Printed in China

Oscar Riera Ojeda Publishers Limited
Unit 1003-04, 10/F.,
Shanghai Industrial Investment Building,
48-62 Hennessy Road, Wanchai, Hong Kong

Production Offices
Suit 19, Shenyun Road,
Nanshan District, Shenzhen 518055, China

International Customer Service & Editorial Questions: +1-484-502-5400

www.oropublishers.com | www.oscarrieraojeda.com
oscar@oscarrieraojeda.com

All rights reserved. No part of this book may be reproduced, stored in a retrieval system, or transmitted in any form or by any means, including electronic, mechanical, photocopying of microfilming, recording, or otherwise (except that copying permitted by Sections 107 and 108 of the U.S. Copyright Law and except by reviewers for the public press) without written permission from the publisher.